LABORERS TOGETHER
THE LAYMAN AND HIS PASTOR

LABORERS TOGETHER

THE LAYMAN AND HIS PASTOR

CHARLES U. WAGNER

Charles U. Wagner.
(see chpt. 2 on plurality.)

REGULAR BAPTIST PRESS
1300 North Meacham Road
Schaumburg, Illinois 60173-4888

Library of Congress Cataloging-in-Publication Data

Wagner, Charles U.
    Laborers together: the layman and his pastor/Charles U.
    Wagner.
    p. cm.
    Bibliography: p.
    ISBN 0-87227-128-5
    1. Laity. I. Title.
BV687.W27 1988   88-31623
253-dc19   CIP

LABORERS TOGETHER: THE LAYMAN AND HIS PASTOR
© 1988
Regular Baptist Press
Schaumburg, Illinois
Printed in U.S.A. All rights reserved

Second printing—1990

Contents

Introduction

Do you ever get the feeling that the pastor and the people in some churches are going in opposite directions? Scripture makes it clear that going in opposite directions is not a workable situation: "Can two walk together, except they be agreed?" (Amos 3:3). On the other hand, there are many areas in which the layman and the pastor do agree. Generally, when the people of a church call a pastor there is new hope and expectancy, and there is a joint desire to see the work of the Lord grow and thrive. Most evangelical churches would agree that one of their most important objectives is to fulfill the Great Commission as set forth in Matthew 28. To be more specific, most pastors and laymen in these churches would maintain that they have some concern for the city or town in which they live and that the only hope for those who live there is the power of the gospel (Rom. 1:16).

But the fact is, the Great Commission is *not* being fulfilled as it should, and the cities and towns in which we live know little or nothing about our churches, many of which have been there for decades. There is a definite disparity between what is professed and what is actually practiced. Whose fault is it? What can be done about it? Ask the pastor, and he might suggest that he is a "one-man army" trying to accomplish church growth in spite of the situation. He is subsequently tired and is even discouraged. Ask the people, and they suggest that they are baffled that they have such a good pastor and yet the church never really seems to grow. In other churches, pastors and laymen are less charitable with each other, and their reasons for lack of church growth range from the location of the church to the need for relocation of the pastor.

The purpose of this book is to help bridge the gap that often exists between the pastor and his people. Rather than placing blame, we will attempt to arrive at workable solutions that help the pastor and people work out their problems. That the best defense is a good offense is unquestioned. But an understanding of the forces on the offense—the leaders, resources, objectives and methods—is vital to victory. Several observations should be made at the outset of our venture toward this victory.

1. It is important for the layman and the pastor to see themselves as servants of the Lord, working together with common goals and objectives, if the job is going to be done.

2. There is often confusion in the distinctions made between the layman and the pastor. Some in Christendom insist that the pastor is the "priest" in the assembly, and his access to God is peculiarly special and specific. To this group, when the pastor speaks he does so with authority. Daring to differ is touching the "Lord's anointed," which is nothing short of dangerous. To state it in the vernacular, the pastor "calls the shots" and "rules the roost" and is the final word.

Others believe that no individual is called of God to pastor a church. To them, "divine call" is a misnomer. Still others allow for an individual pastor but have differing views as to what a pastor is and what his responsibilities are. Is it any wonder that little is being accomplished in many churches? I believe a balanced understanding of the roles and functions of the leaders of a church, and of their relationship with the total congregation, will lead to a healthier-functioning church in keeping with the New Testament example.

3. There are some things that a pastor would like to say to his people but hesitates to do so. Often his hesitation

is due to the delicate, sensitive nature of the matter which could be construed as "self-serving." His hesitation does not mean that he is invertebrate in his convictions. He certainly would be candid and straightforward if the interests of others were in question. He simply chooses not to take the risk of being misunderstood. On the other hand, many sincere laymen express regret for not having taken the lead in helping to solve a problem. Their dilemma was simple: they did not know the problem existed. Such dilemmas frequently are not matters of spirituality but communication. It is a good situation when the pastor and the layman can sit down and honestly and frankly talk about personal issues such as money and the parsonage, as well as general goals and objectives. This is another reason for this book: to help face these needs and issues in order that a better understanding can be enjoyed. As a professor of pastoral theology I have discussed many of these areas with prospective pastors. I now covet the opportunity to share them with the godly layman who has a heart for the ministry and the minister.

4. Finally, I have learned over the years that there are some things about the pastor—for instance, his attitudes, reactions and responses—that perplex the average layman. It is hoped that this book will help overcome such perplexity and bring compatibility and harmony in that most important institution, the local church. Our ultimate goal is to bring glory to the Head of that church, the Lord Jesus Christ. Only if there is harmony in the local church as the servants labor together, doing His bidding, can we expect His coveted commendation.

The church could be likened to a wheel, the hub of which is the Lord Jesus. Everything revolves around Him. Any other center—the pastor, a board, church members—will bring devastating unbalance and ruin. With Christ as the hub, the spokes are the members of that church—including the pastor. As the spokes get closer to the center, the Lord Jesus, they get closer to each other. Only when this desired situation exists will there be balance, and the church will move forward with polish, poise and power.

"To God be the glory" should be the desire of pastor and people as they labor together in the vital vineyard of the local church. "Striving together" is what this book is all about.

CHAPTER ONE
"God Bless My Pastor"

It is a blessing to know that all over the world people pray daily for their pastors. Certainly pastors need prayer, for they daily "wrestle … against principalities and powers" as they shepherd the flock. We should not be surprised that they are the object of much criticism and attack. Certainly one of Satan's strategic moves is to discredit the man leading the battle against his kingdom.

What Is a Pastor?

I am almost reluctant to pose this question. It is like asking what is a father or mother or son. To most of us, the answer is obvious: the pastor is the undershepherd of the flock, the one who ministers the Word and sets the example for the church.

Several words in the Bible speak of this leader we call the pastor: pastor, elder, bishop and angel, or messenger. We will examine each of them .

Pastor

The noun *pastor* is found only once in the New Testament, but it is a clear, significant reference. "And he gave some, apostles; and some, prophets; and some, evangelists; and some, pastors and teachers; For the perfecting of the saints, for the work of the ministry, for the edifying of the body of Christ"(Eph. 4:11, 12). Note that pastors are "given" to the church along with others (apostles, prophets, evangelists). The verb form for pastor is used in Acts 20 where the elders are told to "feed" the church, or tend the sheep. Pastors, then, are shepherds of the flock. Christ is called "the Shepherd and Bishop" of our souls (1 Pet. 2:25). He is the shepherd; pastors are undershepherds, whose responsibility is clear: "Feed the flock of God which is among you" (1 Pet. 5:2).

Bishop

Another name for the pastor is *bishop,* or, in the Greek, *episkopos,* which has the sense of oversight. Scripture speaks very plainly about the qualifications of a bishop.

> Here is a trustworthy saying: If anyone sets his heart on being an overseer, he desires a noble task. Now the overseer must be above reproach, the husband of but one wife, temperate, self-controlled, respectable, hospitable, able to teach, not given to much wine, not violent but gentle, not quarrelsome, not a lover of money. He must manage his own family well and see that his children obey him with proper respect. (If anyone does not know how to manage his own family, how can he take care of God's church?) He must not be a recent convert, or he may become conceited and fall under the same judgment as the devil. He must also have a good reputation with outsiders, so that he will not fall into disgrace and into the devil's trap" (1 Tim. 3:1-7, NIV).

Elder

The words *elder* and *bishop* speak of the same person. Elder speaks of the pastor's person while bishop speaks of his function. The Greek word for elder is presbuteros and was a rather common one to the Jew and Gentile. Barclay writes:

The Jews had their elders, and they traced their origin to the occasion when Moses, in the desert wanderings, appointed seventy men to help him in the task of controlling and caring for the people (Num. 11:16). Every synagogue had its elders, and they were the real leaders of the Jewish community. They presided over the worship of the synagogue; they administered rebuke and discipline where these were necessary; they settled the disputes which other nations would have taken to the law-courts. . . . But more nations than the Jews had an eldership. The presiding body of the Spartans was called the gerousia, which means the board of the elder men. The Parliament of Rome was called the senate, which comes from senex which means an old man. In England the men who looked after the affairs of the community were called the aldermen, which means the elder men. In New Testament times every Egyptian village had its village elders who looked after the affairs of the community. The elders had a long history, and they had a place in the life of almost every community.[1]

It is clear that the pastor has an awesome responsibility as he gives oversight, rule and management in the local church. Frequently, however, he is expected to be even more than is stated in the Word of God. A layman from a Baptist church in Michigan has written:

Man wanted: Minister for Growing Church. A real challenge for the right man! Opportunity to become better acquainted with people! Applicant must offer experience as shop worker . . . office manager . . . educator (all levels), including theologian . . . politician . . . Boy Scout leader . . . children's worker . . . minor league athlete . . .

psychologist . . . vocational counselor. . . psychiatrist . . . funeral director . . . wedding consultant . . . master of ceremonies . . . circus clown . . . missionary . . . social worker. Helpful but not essential: experience as butcher . . . baker . . . cowboy . . . Western Union messenger.

This would be humorous if it were not so very true in many churches. It is clear that what the Bible says about pastors, and what they are often expected to be by the congregation, are quite different indeed. I believe that there are many laymen who, when they become more aware of what is happening, will seek to reverse this unfortunate trend.

How Many Elders in the Church?

When seeking to answer the question of how many elders in the church, we must be ready to move into a maze of laborious speculation. There are many conflicting views on this question. One reason for such a diversity of views is, the work of a pastor seems to be such an impossible task for one man that there should be many elders or pastors sharing in the work. This idea takes many forms.

There Is No One Pastor

First, there is the view that there is no such thing as one who is called of God to be a pastor. Rather, there are several elders in every church who give general oversight. The Plymouth Brethren hold this view; in fact, they take a strong stand against the idea of any person being the pastor. To them there is no divine call to the ministry. The elders are men whom we would refer to as laymen. However, it should be remembered that Scripture makes it clear that the pastor is given to the church, just as the apostle was given to the early church. Pastors are specific, "set apart" people. Also, the word translated de-

sire in the King James Version of 1 Timothy 3:1 implies a definite call of God to the ministry. The New International Version renders it, "If anyone *sets his heart* on being an overseer," which is quite different from a general willingness to fill the position. The New American Standard Version renders it, "If any man aspires to the office of overseer. . . ."

> Kent calls attention to such a strong conviction: It is an office which may be rightfully desired by the believer. Two strong verbs depict the yearning for this office which is commended by Paul. *Orego* means to reach out after, and the middle voice employed here indicates that the subject is reaching after this object for himself. Such a yearning is described by a second verb, *epithumeo*, to desire, to fix the ardor or passion upon a thing. Here it is used in the good sense of strong desire. This godly desire for the responsible task of overseership, if controlled by the Spirit of God, may deepen into a sacred conviction. Such a desire is the motive for preparation in college, Bible school, and seminary. Of course, desire for this task merely for the prestige or honor involved isnot praiseworthy, but if longed for in the will of God is to be commended.[2]

Elders Are Plural

It is often pointed out that when elders are mentioned in Scripture it is always in the plural and therefore there is no real support for the view of the singular pastor. Indeed, the vogue practice today among many is not only to teach the plurality of elders but to insist on it. Often those who hold this view are pastors or congregations who have had little success with individual pastors and conclude that such is neither practical nor workable. The natural answer is that the problem could have been the absence of a divine call in those cases. There seems to be a growing tendency to strike out against authority and strong leadership, to "put down" an authority figure who functions in a Biblical way, reproving and rebuking with the Word.

The argument for many elders in the church based on plurality is not as convincing as it seems on the surface. When Paul said to ordain elders in every city (Titus 1:5), did he mean plurality of elders in every city, or plurality of elders because there is plurality of cities? If every city had one pastor, and there were many cities, it would be proper to refer to elders as plural. Also, we often try to pour the New Testament into our twentieth century mold. Certainly a large church could have had several ordained men pastoring. In some cases there could have been many small churches meeting in houses, each of which would have had an elder. This would still be consistent with the view of a single pastor, divinely called of God. It would not be consistent with the view that there are several elders (like deacons in the Baptist church) who are laymen. It is my position that there is a divinely called pastor, ordained by God, given to the church, who is also called a bishop and an elder.

On the Other Hand . . .

To be fair, it should also be admitted that in many churches the prevalence of overbearing, dictatorial leadership could result in the pendulum swinging away from any kind of singular pastor arrangement. In spite of the fact that Baptists have for centuries held to the priesthood of the believer, some still have an inclination to elevate the pastor to a priestly office and give him an authority and power which, if we understand the New Testament correctly, should reside in the congregation itself. It was never God's plan for one man to make all the decisions with little or no regard for the will of the congregation. An explosive situation frequently results when the shepherd forgets he should lead the flock, not drive them, and that he should be an example to the flock in gentleness and humility.

Back to the Bible

Often the cry is "Let's get back to the Bible" in our church polity. The notion is, forget history, tradition and denominational distinctives and decide by Scripture alone. We agree. But many denominations who have a different view of polity from us would insist that they have Biblical authority for their polity. Why is there so much confusion?

The Pattern of the Early Church

To follow the polity of the early church is not nearly as simple as it sounds. It should be understood that, before the canon of the Scriptures was completed, and while the apostles were still on the scene, church polity was somewhat different from what it is now. We need to see that there is a transition between what was practiced in the early years of the church and what is practiced by the church and still sanctioned by the Lord today. This problem arises frequently among us when we consider the "sign gifts" which were peculiar to the apostolic period. Few of us would argue that tongues are not for today, neither is divine healing (in the apostolic sense of the word), nor prophets, in the true sense of the word of foretelling. There were certain apostolic prerogatives and powers that were characteristic of the early New Testament church.

However, we also need to recognize the differences with regard to church polity and specifically to the ministry. We are not surprised when we find Paul sending Timothy to the church at Philippi (Phil. 2:19–23), nor that he instructed Epaphroditus (v. 25). The instances of Paul's apostolic authority in placing men in various areas are too numerous to mention here. But it is obvious that what was practiced by the apostle in his apostolic injunctions to Timothy and Titus is far from what is practiced today, since we do not have apostles today. Unless we conform to the view of apostolic succession, we are obliged to accept the proposition that church polity in the first century was, at least in its nascent stage, peculiar and unique because there were apostles on the scene. Not until they began to fade out of the picture did we begin to have a situation similar to today's.

The Bridge

As the church developed, individuals began coming to the forefront who might be considered pastors. However, in the developing process there was a transition or intermediate state, which I will refer to as "the bridge."

In his characteristically scholarly style, Lightfoot deals with the development of the Christian ministry from the apostolic in the first century and beyond:[3]

> From the subordinate place, which it thus occupies in the case of St. Paul, the permanent ministry gradually emerged, as the Church assumed a more settled form, and the higher but temporary offices, such as the apostolate, fell away. This progressive growth and development of the ministry, until it arrives at its mature and normal state, will be the object of the following pages to trace.[4]

Homer Kent, in *The Pastoral Epistles,* also speaks of this transition:

The function which Timothy fulfilled in the early church should not be confused with the present-day pastor. Rather, in those formative days of the church he seems to have been one of several who helped to carry out the transition from the times of the apostles to the post-apostolic era of the church.[5]

And Charles Erdman adds:

Timothy and Titus appear to have served as delegates of the Apostle Paul, and as commissioned to represent him in the accomplishment of definite and temporary tasks. They were not apostles, but rather pastors and spiritual leaders, and their activities did not seem to interfere with the self-government of the Christians among whom they sojourned.[6]

Erdman also points out that there were elders, presbyters and bishops during this period, that they were all equal, and that instructions were given by Paul as to their choice, ordination and discipline. What is important to remember at this point is that there was a transition in progress rather than a normal situation, especially with regard to the ministries of Timothy and Titus who, while not pastors in our present sense, were certainly a step in that direction. Erdman says:

The duties of the "bishop" in the early Church, therefore, appear to have been those of spiritual oversight and of religious instruction. The nearest parallel in modern days to this office is that of the "pastor" and it is for this reason that these letters of the Apostle Paul are known as his Pastoral Epistles.[7]

What all of this seems to add up to is that there are strong resemblances between what we would consider the pastor to be today and the principles laid down to Timothy and Titus, except that these men were appointed and sent by the apostle Paul. This period, we believe, is a definite bridge between the apostolic days and our present day. To quote Lightfoot again:

> As the first stage then, the Apostles themselves were the superintendents of each individual church. But the wider spread of the Gospel would diminish the frequency of their visits and impair the efficiency of such supervision. In the second stage therefore we find them, at critical seasons and in important congregations, delegating some trustworthy disciple who would fix his abode in a given place for a time and direct the affairs of the church there. The Pastoral Epistles present this second stage to our view. It is the conception of a later age which represents Timothy as bishop of Ephesus and Titus as bishop of Crete.[8]

The Church Maturing

Of course, during this polity transition we find some churches to be more mature than others. Naturally, the church we would expect to be most fully developed would be the first church, the one organized in Jerusalem. (See Acts 2:41-47.) To examine the church in Jerusalem is to see definite developing steps.

The growth of the church at Jerusalem was phenomenal. With just 120 people in the Upper Room, 3,000 had been saved at Pentecost (Acts 2:41). That group grew by 1,880 more to a total of 5,000 in Acts 4:4. By the time we come to Acts 5, we find a multitude of believers, men and women; this huge group presented the problem necessitating deacons in Acts 6.

In Acts 15, which describes a situation showing the maturity of the church at Jerusalem, James seems to come to the forefront as the nearest thing to what we would consider a pastor today. By no stretch of the imagination could he be considered simply a moderator. After several of the congregation had spoken, including Peter, Paul and Barnabas, James exerted his "pastoral leadership," summed up the situation and made a spiritual judgment (Acts 15:19-21). The apostles, elders and church members concurred with James's decision (vv. 22-27). It is interesting that it was two apostles, Peter and John, along with James, who were considered pillars in the church and gave Paul and Barnabas the right hand of fellowship and commissioned them to go to the heathen (Gal. 2:9). There we have two apostles and what seems to be the pastor making a decision. At the end of Acts, when Paul returned to Jerusalem, we are told that he " . . . went in with us unto James; and all the elders were present" (Acts 21:18). Earlier, when Peter had been divinely released from prison and gone to the house of Mary, and after he had related to the surprised Christians how the Lord had brought him out of prison, he said, "Go shew these things *unto James,* and to the brethren" (Acts 12:17). Paul, relating another instance regarding Peter, talked of Peter's coming from James and eating with the Gentiles (Gal. 2:12). It must be conceded that while there were many elders in the church, and while the apostles still had a degree of authority there, it is no coincidence that James as a singular authority figure is identified with the local church at Jerusalem.

In the next chapter we will see a fuller development of the pastoral ministry, one that is closer to what is practiced in Bible-believing churches today.

End Notes

1 William Barclay, *The Letters to Timothy, Titus, and Philemon* (Philadelphia: Westminster Press, 1960), p. 70. Used by permission.

[2] Homer A. Kent, *The Pastoral Epistles of Paul* (Chicago: Moody Press, 1958), p. 123.

[3] J. B. Lightfoot, *Saint Paul's Epistle to the Philippians* (London: McMillan and Co., 1890), p. 186.

[4] Ibid., pp. 180-269.

[5] Kent, *The Pastoral Epistles,* p. 19.

[6] Charles R. Erdman, *The Pastoral Epistles of Paul* (Philadelphia: Westminster Press, 1923), p. 11.

[7] Ibid., p. 38.

[8] Lightfoot, p. 199.

CHAPTER TWO
The Pastor Is an Angel

Seven Pastors—Seven Churches

When considering the last book of the Bible, Revelation, one should remember that all of the apostles were dead except the writer, the apostle John. Exiled on the Isle of Patmos, John penned seven brief epistles to seven churches. We should not be misled by the brevity of these epistles; they are just as important and pertinent as any other epistle written by an apostle.

In the introduction to these epistles we find the Lord Jesus Christ standing in the middle of seven lampstands. We are told clearly that the lampstands are seven churches (Rev. 1:20). These are local churches and are named in detail in Revelation 2 and 3. Also, in that august description of Christ, we learn that He has in His right hand seven stars. The interpretation of these stars is found in the latter part of chapter 1: "The seven stars are the angels of the seven churches" (Rev. 1:20). It should be understood that the word *angels* here is the Greek word *angelos* which literally means "a messenger" and can refer to either angelic beings or human messengers. C. I. Scofield in the original Scofield Reference Bible writes:

> Angel, "messenger," is used of God, of men, and of an order of created spiritual beings whose chief attributes are strength and wisdom. . . . The word angel is used of men in Luke 7:24; James 2:25; Rev. 1:20; 2:1, 8, 12, 18; 3:1, 7, 14.[1]

The majority of commentators on Revelation, representing various denominational views, confirm that these messengers in Revelation are simply the pastors of the seven churches. We believe that in this passage we have complete support for the view of the singular pastor. Augustus Strong, the Baptist theologian, points out that the bishop in 1 Timothy 3:2 and Titus 1:7 is spoken of in the singular in contrast to the deacons, which are usually spoken of in the plural. He adds:

> So, too, in Revelation 2:1, 8, 12, 18 and 3:1, 7, 14, "the angel of the church" is best interpreted as meaning the pastor of the church; and, if this is correct, it is clear that each church had, not many pastors, but one.[2]

In his excellent book on Revelation, Seiss declares, "The seven stars are the angels (ministers) of the seven churches; and, as such, they are distinct from the candlesticks."[3]

Criswell, in his expository sermons, stresses that the word *angelos* is used several times to mean a man, citing the Hebrew equivalent to the New Testament angelos—kmalaka. He gives as examples Haggai 1:13 and Malachi 2:7. He also cites the New Testament instance of angelos being the minister (Luke 7:24; James 2:25). He writes, "Notice that there is an ordained, ecclesiastical, ministerial office which the Lord God Himself created for his churches."[4]

Later, Criswell adds:

> There is no intimation that this servant, this angelos, this "messenger" of God, is to lord it over God's heritage as though he were a dictator or tyrant, or that he be above being reprimanded and rebuked. What kind of a messenger is he? What kind of an angelos is he? This is the kind that he is: He is a servant of God, to hear the Word

that God speaks, to hear from God. He is an angelos to receive the Word from God, to take it from God's hand, and to deliver it to God's people.[5]

An Epistle to an Angel?

Remember that the word angelos can mean either an angelic being or a human messenger. There are many problems with the idea that the messengers of Revelation 1:20 are angelic beings. While this position is held by those who insist that there is no such thing as an individual pastor, it creates more problems than it solves. Spurgeon speaks to this subject:

> The Apocalyptic title of Angel (Rev. 2:1) means a messenger; and how shall men be Christ's heralds, unless by His election and ordination? If the reference of the word angel to the minister be questioned, we shall be glad to have it shown that it can relate to any one else. To whom would the Spirit write in the church as its representative, but to some one in a position analogous to that of the presiding elder.[6]

To quote Criswell again:

> There is no intimation in Scripture that churches are under the tutelage and instruction of heavenly beings. In the book of Daniel there is a guardian angel over a nation; but, there is no intimation anywhere in Scripture other than that our churches are under the direction and sponsorship of God's appointed servants, the pastors and the preachers whom the holy Spirit sets over His congregations.[7]

Blame It on Your Angel!

I suppose it would be convenient if one could establish that every church has an angel over it (that is, an an-

gelic being), one whom we could hold responsible for anything the church does wrong. But, as Lenski states:

> To allegorize and to make personifications of
> the spirit of the churches is unwarranted.
> These "seven stars" are the pastors of the seven
> churches. They are distinguished from the
> churches as such (lampstands) and yet belong
> to them and in the seven letters are held respon-
> sible for the condition of their churches. . . . But
> the preachers of the church, as the Lord's mes-
> sengers to the church, are in a peculiar way "in
> his right hand" to act as his agents and minis-
> ters in the churches, there to carry out his will
> and his alone.[8]

William R. Newell, in his book on Revelation, states:

> There is no hint, however, that angelic beings
> bear any such relationship to, or responsibility
> for, the assemblies of God in his dispensation.
> Indeed, the very contrary is implied in Colos-
> sians 2:19. Christ is the only Head of the church,
> and the Holy Spirit the only Administrator of
> her affairs on earth. But men are held responsi-
> ble.[9]

With his typically precise presentation, Donald
Grey Barnhouse says in his book on Revelation:

> No angel in Heaven could be held responsible
> for the state of the church on earth. This is clear-
> ly a word to human messengers and reveals
> that even though there is no difference between
> the clergy and the laity, since God commands
> all believers to follow His Word and to walk wor-
> thy of the calling wherewith they have been
> called, there is nevertheless an increased re-
> sponsibility upon those who are spiritual lead-

ers because of the increased opportunity for spiritual service.[10]

Likewise, John Walvoord in his exposition, *The Revelation of Jesus Christ,* says concerning these persons:

> It is more probable that they refer to the leaders in the churches to whom the messages primarily are addressed. The spiritual significance is that these angels are messengers who are responsible for the spiritual welfare of these seven churches and are in the right hand of the Son of Man, indicating possession, protection, and sovereign control. As the churches were to emit light as a lampstand, the leaders of the churches were to project light as stars.[11]

Jonathan Edwards, who stands out as one of the great heroes of the Christian faith in America, once preached a sermon on the true excellency of a gospel minister. Taking the text, "he was a burning and shining light" (John 5:35), he points out that pastors are responsible as lights in the world.

> And so are the ordinary ministers of the gospel called, Rev. 1:16. "And he had in his right hand seven stars." And verse 20, "The mystery of the seven stars which thou sawest in my right hand and the seven golden candlesticks; the seven stars are the angels of the seven churches." Here also ministers of the gospel are implicitly compared to those lamps that enlightened the temple at Jerusalem, upon the tops of the golden candlesticks. . . . [12]

In the sermon, Edwards stresses that ministers are to be lights to the souls of men; as lights they are to refresh and delight the beholders and to be instruments of direction.[13]

One of the finest treatments applying angelos to the messenger-pastor of the churches is given by Richard Trench. "How could holy angels be charged with such delinquencies as are laid to the charge of some of the Angels here (Rev. 2:4; 3:1, 15)?"[14] Trench also answers the suggestion that these were indeed messengers, but only men who were just carrying the message:

> But in answering a letter by a messenger, you write by, you do not usually write to him; nor is it easy to see where is the correspondency between such messengers, subordinate officials of the Churches, and stars; or what the mystery of the relation between them would be; or how the Lord should set forth as an eminent prerogative of his, that he held the seven stars, that is, the seven messengers, in his right hand (Rev. 2:1). The scheme breaks down at every point, and among many lame and feeble shifts must needs be regarded as the lamest and feeblest of all. I again repeat my conviction that in these Angels we are to recognize the bishops of the several churches. So many difficulties, embarrassments, improbabilities, attend every other solution, all of which disappear with the adoption of this, while no others rise in their room, that were not others' interests, often no doubt unconsciously, at work, it would be very hard to understand how any could have ever arrived at a different conclusion.[15]

Finally, Newell, facing the problems identified with any other view, concludes:

> Stars in Scripture stand for those having authority and leadership, also for teachers, both faithful (Dan. 12:3), and false (Jude 13). Inas-

much as the name "angel" is our Lord's interpretation of the symbol star, the name "angel"
cannot be itself another emblem. It must be the
actual name applied by the Lord to certain persons definitely responsible for the state of the
churches addressed.[16]

Does This Mean that Pastors Are Elevated?

When we speak of the seven stars as messenger-
pastors, we must understand that we are not elevating
them to a priesthood different from other believers. Every
child of God is a priest, and no pastor is more of a priest or a
different kind of priest. It should be understood that
while the pastor is in the place of leadership, the head of
the church is Christ, and He is found *in the midst* of the
seven lampstands; He is the final authority. The seven
stars are in His hand, indicating a special responsibility. Not a high position, but a high responsibility is to be emphasized, although certainly it is a privilege to be a pastor
and used of God in that special way in the local church. It
is not that there is an ecclesiastical hierarchy but that
God is holding *men* responsible—not angelic beings.
Criswell says it well:

> He is not talking about passing fancies, mo-
> mentarily significant for the dying hour. He is
> standing in God's sacred place, telling the peo-
> ple what God has to say, how we can be saved
> from our sins, how our souls can be delivered
> from judgment, how some day we must stand
> before God and give an account for the things we
> have done in the flesh.[17]

He continues:

> Their derelictions, their shortcomings, their
> failures, their faults, and their downright sins
> are fearlessly delineated. I could not conceive of

heavenly angels, pure and holy, ministers of lights in the very presence of God—I could not imagine those angels in glory, those messengers of God in heaven, being castigated as Jesus castigates some of these angels over His churches.[18]

Lenski emphasizes the solemnity of the office:

Here is a vision of the office of the holy ministry which every church and every pastor should note. Stars—not human gaslights, or will-o'-the-wisps. Stars—not door mats on which men wipe their feet. Unchanging stars—not men who are always out of breath in an effort to catch up with the changing times of the earth.[19]

Yes, this position as a messenger is a solemn and responsible one, as Joseph Seiss writes:

What a lesson for ministers, as to the holiness of their office, the solemnity of their responsibilities, the necessity of unswerving fidelity, and the exercise of every confidence in their sacred functions. They are in Christ's hand. If they are unfaithful none can deliver them out of that hand; but if true to their position, none can touch them, or quench their light.[20]

While we respect those who hold the opposite view—that these messengers are angelic beings—it is our firm conviction that these seven stars refer to seven individual pastors of seven local churches. Each church has a pastor, and he is responsible to God.

In these past few pages, we have examined what we feel is the ultimate development of the church in the New Testament. First was the apostolic age; second, we saw a bridge between the apostolic and our present day; and finally, we arrived at the settled, stable, normative condition of the church, where each church has a pastor.

A Proper Balance

Scripture clearly states that Christ

> gave some, apostles; and some, prophets; and some, evangelists; and some, pastors and teachers; For the perfecting of the saints, for the work of the ministry, for the edifying of the body of Christ" (Eph. 4:11, 12).

This passage tells us several things: Certain groups were given by God, and this giving was obviously a specific call: apostles were called; the prophets were called; evangelists and pastor-teachers were called; and they were all given by God. Note then that pastors are, first, given to the church. Second, they are messengers from God and the overseers and undershepherds of the flock. However, the purpose of their being given is to perfect the saints for the work of the ministry. In a real sense of the word both pastor and layman are in the ministry. The pastor has been given by God to equip the saints and, together as fellow-priests, they serve the Lord—doing the work of the ministry. It is a wonderful combination, a wonderful partnership, because it is a joint partnership with Christ—the Head of the Church.

End Notes

[1] C. I. Scofield, ed., Scofield Reference Holy Bible (New York: Oxford Press, 1917), notes, p. 1291.

[2] Augustus Hopkins Strong, *Systematic Theology* (Philadelphia: Judson Press, 1907), p. 916.

[3] J. A. Seiss, *The Apocalypse* (London: McArchall, Morgan and Scott, n.d.), p. 41.

[4] W. A. Criswell, *Expository Sermons on Revela-*

tion, vol. 2 (Grand Rapids: Zondervan Publishing House, 1963), p. 30.

[5] Ibid., p. 29.

[6] Charles Haddon Spurgeon, *Lectures to My Students* (Grand Rapids: Zondervan Publishing House, 1977), p. 21.

[7] Criswell, p. 29.

[8] R. C. H. Lenski, *The Interpretation of St. John's Revelation* (Columbus, OH: Wartburg Press, 1943), p. 68.

[9] William R. Newell, *The Book of the Revelation* (Chicago: Moody Press, 1935), p. 33.

[10] Donald Grey Barnhouse, *Revelation: An Expository Commentary* (Grand Rapids: Zondervan Publishing House, 1971), p. 32.

[11] John F. Walvoord, *The Revelation of Jesus Christ* (Chicago: Moody Press, 1966), p. 45.

[12] Jonathan Edwards, *The Works of President Edwards* (London: Leavitt, Trow and Co., 1848), pp. 583-84.

[13] Ibid., p. 584.

[14] Richard Chenevix Trench, *Commentary on the Epistles to the Seven Churches in Asia* (New York: Charles Scribner, 1862), p. 77.

[15] Ibid., pp. 82, 83.

[16] Newell, p. 32.

[17] Criswell, p. 28.

[18] Ibid., p. 29.

[19] Lenski, p. 61.

[20] Seiss, p. 41.

CHAPTER THREE
Calling a Pastor

"What do we do now?" Good question, and one that is often asked when a pastor moves on to another field. This is often a traumatic time for a church because the pastor was loved and appreciated. Now some of us in the church feel that we have been betrayed—even jilted. We feel some animosity toward the other church that "stole" our pastor. After some prayer, however, we usually come to our senses and realize that what is most important is the will of God, and that if the pastor felt it was God's will for him to move on, what else can we do but pray God's blessing on him and wish him the best? Ironically, when the pulpit committee is formed, they will begin to do exactly what they did not appreciate in others—look to other churches for a pastor.

The Pulpit Committee

Pulpit committees are very important in Baptist churches. Actually, if the church were not congregational in polity they would be unnecessary. But, believing that the Bible teaches congregational polity, we do not want a bishop or superintendent appointing our next pastor. So we the congregation appoint a pulpit committee to help seek out a man we can consider for the pastorate. Again, this is a most important committee. Usually the constitution of the church spells out how it is to be formed and who is to be on it. Various departments and a broad range of ages are often represented on the committee to give a good cross section of the church life. However,

there is a tendency to select only older people for this responsibility. I believe that while older people should certainly be included, it is advisable to select a few younger
men—say, age forty-five and under—as well. After all,
this age group may represent the majority age of the
church; also, there is a good chance that they may be
working with the pastor for many years. On the other
hand, care should be exercised that a novice is not select-
ed for the committee. Remember, the most vulnerable
period in the history of a church is when the church is
without a pastor. This is no time for training or experi-
mentation.

Guidelines for the Committee

Once the committee has been formed, the chairman
of the committee should be elected by the committee itself,
unless otherwise specified in the constitution. Each
committee meeting should begin with prayer and each
member should pray, asking for wisdom and seeking
the mind of the Lord. In the first meeting, several
"ground rules" should be established, which we will
consider here.

1. We want God's man for this position and we will
consider the Bible's qualifications for a pastor. We are
aware that the Spirit of God can use the Word of God to direct us to the right man of God to be our shepherd.

2. This should not be a popularity contest. While we
will consider a number of names, we will present one
man at a time to the congregation.

3. Our primary responsibility is to consider various
men and to investigate their qualifications and availability.

4. We will keep our findings strictly confidential in
spite of any pressure that may be placed upon us.

5. We will continually look to God for leading and di-

rection and be sure that we are right with God so we can be proper vessels through whom He can work.

6. We will work resolutely but not hastily or impatiently.

7. We will meet regularly and set aside a time at each meeting for prayer.

8. We understand that it is not our responsibility to call a man. We are representing the church and will leave the final decision to the congregation. We will try not to be discouraged if the congregation does not respond exactly in the manner we desire. We know that these are all areas through which the Spirit works, as He opens and closes doors.

In his excellent book *The Empty Pulpit,* Gillaspie gives a helpful "Procedural Check List" for the church looking for a pastor.

1. Is prayer for guidance being sincerely offered?

2. Is the church ready and willing to be led of the Holy Spirit in its choice?

3. Has prayerful selection been made of an adequate, representative, and dependable pulpit committee?

4. Has a brief but honest self-study been made to determine the needs and related pastoral qualifications?

5. Has an adequate pastoral job specification been drawn up?

6. Has sufficient and up-to-date information been gathered concerning the church so that intelligent answers can be given to the candidate's questions?

7. Has it been agreed that the needs of the candidate and his family will also be carefully investigated and evaluated in the total picture?

8. Has the committee determined to first con-

sider the qualifications of men best suited to the needs of the church?

9. Has the committee agreed to present to the church only one man at a time?

10. Has it been agreed that careful and thorough investigation and inquiry will be the essential policy?

11. Has the committee agreed to narrow the list of possibilities to a few worthy and desirable men to thoroughly investigate?

12. Is it understood that this investigation will be done before the man is invited to visit the church?

13. Have the possible sources for names and information been determined and agreed upon?

    a. Denomination sources

    b. Friends and members of the church

    c. Fellow pastors

    d. School and other records

    e. Present and past pastorates of candidate

    f. Candidate himself

14. Have visits been made to hear the man preach in his own pulpit and to view the work of his present pastorate?

15. Has a tentative outline been made as to the procedure of the candidate's visit to the church so that the visit will be meaningful and efficient?

16. Has the procedure of submitting a candidate to the church along with his qualifications been outlined so that sufficient information is given for an intelligent vote by the people?

17. Have the contents of the call letter been tabulated and outlined so that sufficient information will be given the candidate for his serious consideration?[1]

What Do We Look for in a Pastor?

What kind of man are you looking for? This should be one of the first major considerations by the congregation. Members of the pulpit committee ought to form a "check list" as to the ideal person. Let's go over some suggestions and consider some questions.

1. A person who is doctrinally sound. It is possible to invite a man who is very charismatic and a good preacher but who does not stand with the church in its doctrinal position. Woe to the church who finds out too late that this is the case. The doctrinal statement of a church is spelled out in its constitution, and any candidate ought to agree with it *without any reservation* before he is invited to come.

2. One who meets the Biblical qualifications. It is possible for one to hold right doctrinal truth yet not be "fitted" for the ministry. Read carefully 1 Timothy 3:1-7. Study it, examining every qualification and its meaning. Discuss the meaning of each qualification, using word study books and commentaries. You cannot be too careful. (See chapter 4 for further thoughts on this.)

3. One who is baptistic. It stands to reason that if you are a Baptist church the one you call ought to be a Baptist and hold to the Baptist distinctives. I never cease to wonder how a person who is not a Baptist gets into a church and ultimately disappoints the congregation when he tries to make it undenominational. Such a situation reflects deception on the part of the candidate and carelessness on the part of the pulpit committee. Here are the Baptist distinctives:

Bible as authority
Autonomy of each local church
Priesthood of the believer
Two ordinances: baptism, the Lord's Supper
Saved, baptized church membership
Two offices: pastor and deacons

Security of the believer

4. One who is evangelistic. This is important. After all, it reflects obedience to the Great Commission. Has the candidate shown through his personal experience that he has a burden for souls? Does he preach the gospel? Is he a soul-winner? Does he believe in training others to join him in winning the lost? Does he give an invitation in services? The importance of these considerations merits their being carefully weighed. Then your conclusion should be that certainly you want a man who is evangelistic.

5. One who is dispensational. Admittedly, some of these suggestions reflect my position. If a person is a premillennialist and believes in the distinction between Israel and the church and is looking for the Rapture, the return of Christ for His church, he is a dispensationalist. A great many problems can be avoided if this is found out at the outset.

6. One who is a separatist. The candidate's position on both church and personal separation is important. How does the candidate feel about cooperative evangelism? What is his position on the ecumenical movement? What degree of cooperation would he give to the councils of churches and ministerial groups? Does he believe in personal separation? How does he feel about the theater, the dance, social drinking?

7. One who agrees with and will support the church covenant. (Ask if the candidate, if called, would make an effort to eliminate this covenant.)

8. One who does not have "hobby horses," that is, topics he constantly harps on. (Beware of any sign of this in the interview.)

9. What is the candidate's position on divorce and remarriage? How does he feel about mixed marriages (that is, marriages in which one is a Christian and the other is not)? Will he marry two unsaved people?

10. How does the candidate feel about projects to raise money (suppers, bazaars, etc.)?

11. It is important to know something about the candidate's educational background. Where did he go to school? How does he feel now about the school's doctrinal position? Would he send students there?

12. Questions regarding the candidate's former pastorates are in order. Where has he ministered? How long did he stay, and would he be willing to discuss reasons for leaving? How does he feel about his ministry in those places?

13. Fellowship questions are also in order. For instance, how does he feel about the General Association of Regular Baptist Churches? Does he have an any reservations about its practices, positions and publications? Will he work with the Fellowship, its schools and agencies? What would it take for him to exercise leadership to leave the Fellowship? Is his position detached? Mildly cooperative? Or is he in wholehearted support? These questions may seem trivial to some, but they are important. While the Fellowship is known for being just that, a *fellowship* of independent Baptist churches, a church will frequently call a man who has no intention of maintaining that affiliation. Of course, we respect the right of pastor and people to determine their own future and affiliation. But it is proper for a church to know any agenda he may have and, should they desire, to let this be a determining factor in their decision to call him.

Pulpit Considerations

Because the Bible is so important in our churches, the way it is preached and taught is important as well. One very important area of consideration, then, is the pulpit ministry of the pastor. I have often made the statement to seminarians that one's congregation could forgive him for almost anything except not being able to preach the Word and communicate spiritual truths properly. Frankly, noting how some congregations dearly love their pastors in spite of a lack of pulpit ability, I have come to modify that statement somewhat (although it is still puzzling to me).

Frequently, the call of a man is based solely on one or two sermons preached during the candidating process. This, of course, is a mistake. There is a difference between one's ability to deliver one rather acceptable message and a consistent pulpit ministry. It is therefore wise for the pulpit committee to take several opportunities to hear the candidate, preferably in the place where he currently ministers. Then, a short series of messages from the candidate at the seeking church is better than a "trial Sunday." Again, careful inquiries as to where the candidate has ministered and what kind of pulpit ministry he enjoyed there are in order.

Gillaspie helps us again in his book *The Empty Pulpit,* in which he lists questions to use in evaluating the pulpit ministry.

1. Is there a sense of spiritual thoroughness to his preaching? Is it Bible centered?

2. Is there more than elegance of manner or elocutionary brilliance? Is there depth to his sermons?

3. Is his preaching powerful in conveying spiritual truths to hearts and minds?

4. What ability does he have as a teacher?

5. Where is his strength in the pulpit? As an evangelist, recruiter, teacher?

6. Is there breadth to his preaching? Does he reach the young as well as the old?

7. Is the Scriptural basis of his preaching broad in its scope, or is it nearly all in one area or division?

8. Do his sermons inform, teach, uplift, challenge?

9. Are his sermons clear? Easily followed by the young?

10. Does he have any unpleasant or repulsive mannerisms?

11. Besides preaching, can he lead people into genuine worship?

12. What attitude does he have toward music in the church?

13. Is his preaching expository, textual, topical, or a mixture?

14. Does he concentrate on social problems per se, or does he relate these to his expository preaching in a vital approach?

15. Does he honestly deal with current social concerns from a Biblical viewpoint?[1]

Where Do We Look for a Pastor?

1. To the Lord, of course! There should be much fervent, serious prayer by the individual pulpit committee members in their own devotions as well as by the committee when they meet. The spirit of prayer should pervade *the entire congregation.*

2. Trusted friends. Frequently a neighboring pastor can give a list of names that is helpful.

3. The home office. If the church belongs to a fellowship, contacting the home office could prove productive. They will give you only as much help as you desire; but their advice is usually wise. They may know men who would fit in well, since they would know both the church and available candidates.

4. Schools and agencies. Most seminaries and Bible colleges have a placement department and know of men presently in the ministry who may be seeking the mind of God about changing churches. A letter to the school or agency reflecting your burden, the kind of man you are

looking for and some information about your church could be the first step toward finding the right shepherd for the flock.

5. Men well known and respected in the Fellowship. Generally there are several leaders whose advice and counsel you respect. Contact these men and ask them to prayerfully consider submitting names of possible candidates.

6. Names sent by candidates. I have left this as a last source because I feel that it deserves to be last. Generally the person who volunteers for the job and tells you he feels led to your church is not the best candidate. There could be some exceptions to this, but if so they are just that— exceptions. Go easy here.

It is a good practice for the committee to be agreed before they present a candidate to the church. Remember, to a great degree the committee will be a cross section of the people. If there is anything less than a unanimous feeling among the committee, they should be cautious in recommending a candidate. Again, this is one of the most important decisions that will be made in the church's life. Careful, prayerful attention should be given each step of the way. Remember, the Lord is with you and wants to direct you to the man of His choosing.

End Notes

[1] Gerald W. Gillaspie, *The Empty Pulpit* (Chicago: Moody Press, 1975), pp. 80-81.

[2] Ibid., p. 88.

CHAPTER FOUR
Let the Bible Help You Choose a Pastor

Without a doubt the most important single passage that deals with the qualifications of a pastor is 1 Timothy 3. It is wise, therefore, to carefully study this passage and look for a man who has the qualifications listed. Let's do just that. Remember that we are reading what God the Holy Spirit told Paul to write concerning the pastor. He directed him, and us, as to just what God considers important with respect to this high office.

The Pastor's Testimony

How the pastor is perceived is important. It *does* matter what people think about him, both Christians and the world. He should, he *must*, have a testimony that is without question. Note that in addition to his testimony with respect to the church, "he must have a good report of them which are without" (1 Tim. 3:7). "A bishop then must be blameless" (v. 2) might serve as a basis for this qualification or as a "caption" or heading for the other qualifications. Someone has pointed out that the first half of the qualifications in 1 Timothy 3 is positive and the second primarily negative. Hendriksen points out:

> It must not escape our attention that the very first and the very last of the eight positive requirements describe the qualified person's relation to his *family*. That relationship is again

emphasized in connection with the deacons. Paul (and the Holy Spirit speaking through Paul) must have regarded this family-relationship as being of great importance.[1]

Blameless

"A bishop then must be blameless." Let's be clear that the word *blameless* does not mean *sinless*. While sinlessness is certainly the aim of every Christian, we as a church will not find a perfect man. If blameless did mean sinless there would be reason to take the passage lightly, and we would assume that there are exceptions to every qualification because we cannot attain that state of sinlessness. When I pointed out to a friend, on one occasion, that a certain person should not be in the ministry because he was not blameless, the friend asked, "Are you blameless?" The obvious implication was that I was not perfect, and who can be. But the answer was, and should be (and without pride), "yes" when answered by every pastor, because the word means to be *above and beyond reproach*. It means *irreprehensible* or *unassailable*.

> Enemies may bring all manner of accusations, but these charges are proved to be empty whenever fair methods of investigation are applied. With the church and in accordance with the rules of justice, this man not only has a good reputation but deserves it.[2]

Kenneth Wuest says about this word *blameless:*

> The word "blameless" is *anepilambano*, made up of *lambano*, "to take," and *epi*, "upon"; thus, the compound means "to lay hold upon," and all this is stated in the negative by having prefixed to it the letter, Alpha, making the entire word mean, "one who cannot be laid hold upon." That

is, a bishop must be of such a spotless character that no one can lay hold upon anything in his life which would be of such a nature as to cast reproach upon the cause of the Lord Jesus. He presents to the world at large such a Christian life that he furnishes no grounds for accusation. Expositors says: "It is not enough for him to be not criminal; he must be *one against whom it is impossible to bring any charge of wrong doing such as could stand impartial examination.* He must be *without reproach* (R. V.), irreprehensible (Trench)."[3]

The Husband of One Wife

While there are many views on the phrase, "the husband of one wife," the most sensible seems to be that he is to be a *one-woman man.* Wuest says that it can mean a one-wife sort of a husband.[4] He loves one woman; that's his nature. Well does Hendriksen say:

It is stipulated that in this marital relationship he must be an example to others of faithfulness to his one and only marriage-partner. Infidelity in this relationship is a sin against which Scripture warns repeatedly. That this sin and those related to it (sexual immorality in any form) were of frequent occurrence among the Jews and certainly among the Gentiles, is clear from ever so many passages. . . . Accordingly, the meaning of our present passage (1 Tim. 3:2) is simply this, that an overseer or elder must be a man of unquestioned morality, one who is entirely true and faithful to his one and only wife; one who, being married, does not in pagan fashion enter into an immoral relationship with another woman.[5]

Vigilant

The word *vigilant* is the Greek word *nephalion* and means to be calm. Vincent includes "wise caution." We are talking about a "collected" person who is not easily upset and who does not make spur-of-the-moment decisions, later regretted.

Sober

The idea here is that the pastor is serious and earnest. This qualification tells of his judgment and that he is not moved by fads or false doctrine.

Of Good Behavior

The simplest explanation for "of good behavior" is "orderly." The word *dignified* would also not be a bad definition. The Greek word *kosmion* is used, from *kosmeo*, which means to arrange, and *kosmos*, world. So his sermons, his habits, his general lifestyle are characterized by orderliness rather than by chaos and confusion.

Given to Hospitality

Hospitality was most important in New Testament times when Christians needed Christians in view of the persecution that prevailed. But even today it has a real application. The pastor should be a people person, not someone who is withdrawn and has no interest in the needs and problems of others. He is to be a real "overseer," a pastor with a heart.

Apt to Teach

The pastor should be able to communicate truth to others. Teaching is very important in a pastor's ministry if he is going to disciple people and see growth in their lives. He must be "rightly dividing the Word of truth" in such a way that there will be spiritual progress in the life of each member of the congregation. Specific skills in this area are most important.

Not Given to Wine

The pastor should be most careful in his social habits. Wine in Bible times was certainly not what it is today, but even then this injunction was important.

No Striker

The word *striker* speaks of a bruiser, one who is a real fighter. It is no compliment to say a pastor has a fiery temper he cannot control. The church is no place for a leader who is quarrelsome and contentious. We can suggest only that a person's record be examined in this respect. If you find that a man has had trouble getting along with his deacons, friends and church members, he is not likely to be any different in the new church.

Patient

We are talking here about a gentle (*epiekes*) person, one who is yielding and who exercises forbearance. He is not domineering and demanding. Thayer defines patience as "mildness, fairness, sweet reasonableness." We need more of this kind of person in the pastorate.

Not a Brawler

A pastor should not go around with a chip on his shoulder, looking for someone to knock it off. He should not be "offensively aggressive," always insisting on his rights as pastor.

Not Covetous

The area of money, and money loving, is a serious one. No pastor should be in the ministry for the money. Money matters must be kept in perspective. While it is proper to talk about his needs, and for him to be "up front" about his obligations, they should not be the most important consideration. Beware of one who is more interested in benefits and what you can do for him than how he can serve the Lord in the church.

One that Ruleth Well His Own House

The reason for this as a qualification is, "For if a man know not how to rule his own house, how shall he take care of the church of God?" (1 Tim. 3:5). The attitude of the pastor toward his wife and children, and their behavior, is telling. The word *rule* means to superintend. The word *well* seems to convey the idea of "beautifully, finely, excellently" (*kalos*). There is a dignity and respect that is given to the pastor by his family. He presides over them in a loving way and they respond favorably to his leadership.

Not a Novice

The pastor should not be a new convert. The reason is given, " . . . lest being lifted up with pride he fall into the condemnation of the devil" (1 Tim. 3:6). The thought here is that to promote, or elevate, a person to this place of leadership would incite pride. There is no place for pride in the work of the Lord.

A Good Report of Them which Are Without

His reputation is important. After all, he will be preaching with a view of people of the world coming to Christ. If he has a poor testimony, the church will suffer, and they will not be able to fulfill their task, which includes reaching the world for Christ. He should be one who pays his bills, who handles himself with dignity and sobriety. He should not be a clown or a joke to the world.

By now you can easily see that we are looking for a very special man, although he is not a superman or a perfect man. But these basic requirements in 1 Timothy 3 are most important if the church is going to be blessed of God and reach its full potential. Notice that nothing is said about a charismatic personality in this passage. Nor do we find him a "high-class" person who can impress the elite and appeal to the businessman. We are not looking for a "Madison Avenue" executive who, with his entrepreneurial spirit, can work miracles. Sometimes when I am contacted to recommend pastors I am asked if the person would do well on television or radio. We are often more interested in a glamorous man than we are a holy man! This is not to our credit. As we read and reread this list of qualifications, we may take ourselves out of the Hollywood mold and look for a man who can be used by the Holy Spirit in meeting the needs of the church and leading the church on to victory.

End Notes

[1] William Hendricksen, *New Testament Commentary: Exposition of the Pastoral Epistles* (Grand Rapids: Baker Book House, 1957), p. 121.

[2] Ibid., pp. 120-121.

[3] Kenneth S. Wuest, *The Pastoral Epistles in the Greek New Testament* (Grand Rapids: Wm. B. Eerdmans Publishing Co., 1952), pp. 52-53.

[4] Ibid.

[5] Hendriksen, p. 121.

CHAPTER FIVE
Initial Steps in Finding God's Man

Continue to pray! In each step of the candidating process, prayer should be an incessant practice.

Once you have some idea of the kind of man you are looking for and have several sources from which to receive names, you are ready to take the initial steps in contacting candidates.

Let's assume that you have many names—perhaps twenty or twenty-five. Some of the names can be eliminated so that you end up with a list of four or five men you can consider as serious candidates. Narrowing down the list will not be as difficult as you think. It is also possible that one or two that are eliminated now will be seriously considered later. All of this is in the hand of the Lord as He directs by opening and closing doors.

You may wish to send a letter to all twenty men. If so, it should be general and it should be clear that you are in the nascent stage of seeking a man. Honesty at all times is the best policy. To be "up front" with the people you contact will bring spiritual blessings and a peace of mind that you are not manipulating or playing with their lives.

Five Possibilities

Let's say that after several weeks of general inquiry, five men seem to emerge as good possibilities. Now what? You might submit another letter showing added interest and asking more pertinent questions. A phone call

51

might also be in order. If tapes of the person's presaching are available, you might ask for the sermon preached the past Sunday. Another practice is to visit the church where the man is pastoring. This should be done discreetly. To have five or six men walk into a church and sit together, taking notes when a pastor is preaching, could be embarrassing. If three men are assigned to go, they might go at different times or, if they visit at the same time, they might choose to sit in different places. Remember, you are not being deceptive; you are merely trying not to be disruptive or cause embarrassment. An informal meeting with the pastor on a Sunday afternoon could prove helpful. But if this is done, you should contact him a week before and inform him that you are going to visit the church and ask for some time with him that day.

If you feel strongly about one of the four or five men, you might want to invite him to preach on a Sunday. Make it clear that he is not a candidate at that point. He should be made aware of the entire candidating process. Sometimes we laugh at this and call it a Baptist game that is played and that actually he *is* candidating. But the practice is not a bad one; it is done to give the man an opportunity to look over the work and get the general "feel" of the congregation and the area. Also, the church can be exposed to his ministry without making any commitment. In spite of the criticism it gets, this step is not that bad of a practice if it is done with integrity and honesty.

Before the Candidating

It should be remembered that once you ask a man to candidate, you are taking one of the final steps in this process. You should not make this move until you are rather sure that, all things being equal, he will be presented to the church. To ask a person to candidate is to say to the congregation, We have thought this through, we have done our homework and, having considered many men, this is the one that we are presenting for your prayerful consideration. So you see how serious a matter it is. Before actually calling him to candidate, the pulpit committee should review their steps and his qualifications. Does he meet the criteria that has been established? If not, how important is the difference? What seem to be his strengths, his weaknesses? Does he come recommended by his peers? By his former churches? Where has he served? How long did he stay there? Was his ministry there blessed by God? What patterns seem to emerge once you examine his ministry and the churches he has pastored? Would he feel comfortable with the stand your church takes? Or does he merely have an "I can live with it" attitude? (The latter is very dangerous.) You have examined him from Scripture, you have talked with him, prayed with him, heard him preach, you have related to him—are there any "gut feelings" that something is still not quite right? That might sound rather strange, but you cannot be too careful. Is there a unanimous feeling on the part of the board about this brother? Do you sense that God is directing?

The Visit to Candidate

Now you are ready to ask the brother to come and be considered a candidate. This can be an exciting time. Several things can be done at this point.

1. Make arrangements for lodging. I would suggest that you ask both the man and his wife to come and any children they may have at home. My advice is to put them in a motel, not in a private home, so that they can get proper rest and have the privacy they need.

2. Give them a copy of the constitution and other information regarding the church, such as a financial statement, membership figures, anything unique about the church, and something of the history of the church. Also, a map of the city would be helpful.

3. Try to anticipate and have answers ready for any questions he may have. What is the projected growth of the church? Of the Sunday School? What is their vision for missions? For a Christian school?

4. Provide a history of the city, its growth patterns, its industry and its areas of interest.

5. Show them the parsonage—inside and out—if there is one.

6. Go over the housing, the salary, the benefits (health, pension, etc.).

At all times you will want to make the candidate feel at ease and comfortable. You will want to give him a good picture of the church and its outreach. You might ask him to be with you in meetings for two or three days if possible, preferably Sunday through Wednesday. Frequently a person will have one or two good sermons that will help a congregation reach a decision about him. However, this person will be preaching from two to five times a week, preparing several sermons and, as we stated earlier, in fairness to him and to the church, a more extended time of hearing him preach is best.

Meeting with the Candidate

During this candidating period is the time to meet with the candidate and ask serious questions. Certainly he ought to meet with the pulpit committee. He should also meet with the deacons and trustees for a time of fellowship and questions. If he can stay for a few days, a luncheon with the various key leaders in the church is in order. Consideration should be given to meeting with the church staff, the Sunday School staff and any other group or individuals vital to the ongoing of the church. Of course, there are limitations, but these meetings can be held in informal settings, at dinners, after the evening service or at other convenient times.

Yes, this can be a stressful time, but it can also be a blessed time. You are seeing the church in action. You are sensitive to the will of God and His leading. Someday you may look back on these days with real fondness.

Possibly you have detected a spirit of caution and negativism in what I have just written. As a pastor for over thirty years, I have seen many local churches move through this process rather lightly and hastily and, as a result, found themselves repenting. There are thousands of good men who are God-fearing, Spirit-filled servants of the Lord, worthy of your consideration. But, at the same time, there are some hirelings, men who can give the right answers and make their way into the hearts of the people. Also, there are some good men whose spirituality cannot be questioned, but who apparently have not received a divine call to the ministry, and everything they touch seems to die. While they are to be loved and respected, the fact remains that you want the right man for your church; therefore you cannot be too careful in this sacred and solemn process. God bless you as you seek His will.

CHAPTER SIX
Getting Ready for the New Pastor

The church constitution will spell out what the congregational vote must be before a call can be extended to a candidate. The lowest percentage of a vote is frequently stipulated at 75 percent; sometimes more, rarely less. It is important to comply with the constitution; it should never be overridden. If a certain amount of time is stipulated between the candidate's coming as a candidate and the vote, it should be carefully respected, even though it might prove inconvenient to the candidate or seem unreasonable because of the certainty of everyone that he is the right man. The vote should be by ballot and the results announced. Be sure to spend time praying in the days and weeks before the vote and to have a spirit of unity and oneness of mind that the will of God is paramount.

There is the possibility that if the vote is not 90 percent or better, the candidate will not accept the call. You should not be disappointed if he does not feel that a 75 percent vote is a mandate. Honesty is important here. When he is informed as to the vote he should be told the actual vote. Often a church will ask the whole congregation to vote unanimously, after a three-fourths majority has been registered, as an indication that the whole church is willing to go with the majority. This practice is not necessarily bad. It shows that while a person voted against the candidate, he is spiritual enough to respect the general mind of the congregation. Unless there are glaring reasons and deep-rooted convictions as to why he should not stand with the majority, this spirit is commendable. However, if this step is taken, the candidate should be so informed. To be told the vote was unanimous when the actual first vote was not is not fair to him.

His Response

Do not expect the candidate to respond immediately. Even though he may feel rather certain that if a call is extended he will accept, he will want to pray about the matter and be sure it is the will of God for him and his family. He may seek the counsel of a trusted friend. He may even want to share the matter with the chairman of the board in his present church and ask for prayer. You will probably hear within two weeks; generally sooner. If he responds negatively, you must accept this as a closed door and the will of God. If he responds affirmatively, there is yet much work to do in the process of preparation. It is important that you work with your future pastor with respect to the announcing of his coming. For example, he may give the chairman of the pulpit committee an affirmative answer but ask for a week or more before it is announced to the church. The reasons are obvious; he will want time to inform his own people. It will harm his testimony, and perhaps even jeopardize his relations with the new work, if this is not honored. Extreme care should be taken here.

Yes, He Is Coming

When the good news comes, you will want to let the church know as soon as possible. Information should be sent to the local newspaper. You may want to send out a letter to the membership and other interested parties (missionaries, etc.). Again, be sure that you speak with your future pastor as to how and when the announcements should be made.

Where Will He Live?

Now that you know he is coming and have some idea of when he will arrive, another natural question is, Where will he live? By now a great deal of thought should have gone into this matter. If the church has a parsonage and the new pastor has agreed to live there, there is the matter of getting it ready. Will it be redecorated? If so, he and his wife should be consulted as to the color of rooms, the carpet (if it is to be replaced) and any other major changes. This preparation should be taken care of soon after the call. While the church might be pressed financially, I would suggest that cuts be made other places in the church expenses so that adequate housing can be offered to the pastor. Will the present house be adequate, given the size of his family and his individual needs? Will his study be in the house? If so, it should be prepared accordingly. In some cases, it might make good sense to buy another house. These are all important options. You will find that care and interest in these areas will be to the benefit of the congregation. For the pastor and his family to be comfortable and unconcerned about these matters will mean that he can give himself to his major task: pastoring his flock.

Buying His Own Home

While we will deal with this subject more thoroughly in another chapter, it is important at this point to suggest that if your church is one where it is customary for the pastor to provide his own home, you could consider helping him with a loan. It is possible that he has been living in parsonages for years, or that he does not have sufficient equity in the house where he presently lives, and we all know how difficult it is to buy a house without a down payment. Or, if the down payment is small, the monthly payments will be large and possibly out of his range. Some churches have anticipated this possibility and agree to lend their pastors enough for a down payment, interest free. Then, at a later date, the pastor can pay back the loan. He can do it on a monthly basis, or start a year after the loan was made or even wait until the house is sold, should he move to another area. Other churches charge a small amount of interest.

Certainly, some of these areas are sensitive and the pastor will often be reluctant to speak of them for fear of causing misunderstanding. But he will want to "provide for his own house" in a way that is honoring to the Lord. The church should not just assume that he can make it without help. Nor should everyone assume that someone else is handling this matter. Someone on the board of trustees or in some official capacity ought to take the first step in handling the pastor's housing. It will help assure a good, smooth beginning in the relationship with the new pastor.

Keep the Pastor Informed

It could be several weeks or even months before the new pastor arrives. This period will give you time to get things ready. Naturally he will be thinking about his new church and its activities, probably more than you realize. After all, what is going on at the church is of value and interest to him even though he is not yet there. So be sure to keep him informed with regular letters and bulletins and periodic phone calls. Efforts should be made to maintain "status quo" in the church until he arrives. Let me share two instances in my own personal experience to show what I mean.

In one of the churches I pastored it was decided that some things should be "cared for" before I arrived, so a constitutional committee was appointed to change some items in the constitution to make it easier. Believe me, this does not make it easier. First, a good policy is to go very slowly in ever changing the constitution, and certainly do not try to do it without a pastor. In another church the missionary policy was changed in the interim between pastors. What a mistake! Often there is a "restlessness" in a congregation when it is between pastors, resulting in grave mistakes made in church meetings. Satan knows that the church is most vulnerable when it has no shepherd, and he will do everything he can to cause confusion and chaos during this period. A policy of "wait until the pastor comes" is a good one. He will discuss change and revision with the congregation in due time.

The Other Extreme

I think the only time I developed an ulcer was when I was pastoring two churches. I had given notice to one that I felt led to leave, and I had accepted another. It was hard for me to say good-bye to the church where I had pastored for so many years. I loved those people; now it was important that I close out my ministry there in a way honoring to the Lord. But the church to which I had been called was having problems and wanted my input. The problems were complex, and making decisions without actually being there was difficult. The whole situation was complicated by the fact that I was, in effect, pastoring two churches. Again, the rule is to keep the pastor informed, keep "status quo" in the church as much as possible, and do not expect the pastor to make decisions before he arrives. Common sense is the rule. Once we see the total picture of the pastor in transition, it is easy to understand ways and means of helping him during this important time of adjustment.

Here at Last

It has been a long time since the last pastor read his resignation. At first, everybody wondered what the church would do. But the long weeks and months that have expired have been times of learning and growth, and somehow the value of a pastor has become more apparent since the church has been without one. On the other hand, the fact that the church has done as well as it has shows that the real head of the church is Christ Himself. But even now, grateful that an undershepherd has finally come, some of the people still doubt as to how it will all work out. After all, no one knows the new man very well, and certainly he does not know all about them and their idiosyncrasies. But they are helped by the fact that the Lord is in this, and He knows them all, and He knows what they need. So, they thank the Lord that He has sent a choice servant and determine that they are going to do all they can to make his ministry a fruitful and productive one—one in which they all can grow spiritually.

CHAPTER SEVEN
Who's Pulling the Wagon?

When I was a young boy, I enjoyed spending the summers with my grandfather and a whole array of aunts and uncles in Tennessee. Life's greatest adventure was to look for arrowheads in the fields or spend an afternoon at ol' Yellow Creek, where I learned to dive before I learned to swim. Of course part of the excitement was the animals, and I especially enjoyed those not-so-hurried rides to church on the old flatbed wagon. Grandad would hitch up two mules (the same ones that had been plowing the fields just yesterday), and we would all hop on the flatbed to ride to the old country church. I happened to be the brakeman, which involved manipulating a long pole near the rear wheel. What memories.

One day I got to thinking about that wagon. With all its cracks and creaks it wasn't a bad means of transportation. Not fast, but steady. Yet it was only as steady as the two-mule power that gave it the necessary pull.

Let's Get on the Wagon

A great many people get the idea that the major purpose of church is to "get on the wagon" and ride with the rest of the congregation. If the analogy seems deficient, I would further suggest that the pastor is frequently "harnessed up" and equipped to give the church all the movement it is going to get as it inches on through history. You will have to use a little imagination here, but do you get the picture? The pastor is pulling, the people are riding and the wagon is moving—ever so slowly. Then, someone inquires why the wagon is not moving as fast as it once did. "Why, we are hardly moving at all," he exclaims. "I just don't know why we are not making more progress. Maybe it's time for a change!"

Yes, a change is in order, but not a change of pastors. After all, it hardly helps for several deacons to be pulling the wagon the other way and exclaiming, "We never did it that way before!"

At this point the reader may be suspicious as to the conclusion in this analogy. Is the pastor to be in the driver's seat, directing the people who are pulling the wagon? No, the fact is, we *all* need to be pulling the wagon, and a careful examination of the plan of God for the operation of the church and those involved in it will show this to be the case. Let's look at some classic Scriptural passages for answers.

The Perfecting of the Saints

One of the clearest passages in the Bible with respect to who should be doing the work of the ministry is Ephesians 4:11 and 12.

"And he gave some, apostles; and some, prophets; and some, evangelists; and some, pastors and teachers [or pastor-teachers] . . ." (Eph. 4:11). Four categories are offered here. The first two, apostles and prophets, were foundational and peculiar to the early church. The apostles were limited to the Twelve, plus Paul, the apostle to the Gentiles. They had to have been witnesses of the Resurrection (Acts 1:15-22) and to have seen Christ after the Resurrection (1 Cor. 9:1, 2). Clearly, the Bible teaches the apostles were foundational (Eph. 2:20). Prophets were those who proclaimed the Word of God in the early church (Acts 28). They played a special part in what we might call "occasional inspiration" until the Bible was complete and they were therefore no longer needed. The next two, the evangelist and the pastor-teacher, are with us today. The evangelist deals with "dead" men, preaching new life in Christ, and is used as a soul-winner (seeing dead men live) and a church-planter. The evangelists were probably itinerant preachers quite similar to our home missionaries. Philip was promoted from a deacon to an evangelist (Acts 21:8). The pastor-teacher is one who shepherds and teaches; the two positions seem to go together. He is to feed the church of God (Acts 20:28). Remember that the evangelist and the pastor-teacher are *gifts* of Christ to the church. Note their purpose. ". . . He gave . . . some pastors and teachers; For the perfecting of the saints, for the work of the ministry . . . (Eph. 4:11, 12).

Three words stand out in this passage. Note, first, the word saints. It is the saints, not only the shepherds, who are doing the work of the ministry. The saints are "perfected"—that is, equipped—to do the work. The word *perfected* is from a root word that means to unite or bind together. The verb form of the word is rendered "to mend" (Matt. 4:21), to "render complete or perfect"(Luke 6:40; 2 Cor. 13:11) and to "prepare" or "render fit" for the work (Heb. 10:5; 13:21). It is clear that the pastor is to put the armor on the saint so that the saint can join the pastor in the battle. The saint is helping the pastor to "mend the nets" so he can join the pastor in "fishing for men." The saint is being equipped so he can join the pastor in doing the "work of the ministry." How different this is from the idea that the ministry is the job of the pastor! No, it is not the pastor *alone* who is pulling the wagon: it is the pastor and *the people*. When a church grows and advances, when it matures, it is because it is impacted by the ministry of the pastor *and* the people. This concept is the basis of the success of any church, and it is perhaps the most important concept of this book.

Great People in a Great Church

Most of my life as a pastor was spent in the great Pacific Northwest. I remember meeting with the board of the little church in Richland, Washington, my first pastorate there, and explaining to them the Biblical concept of "equipping the saints" so we could all be involved in the ministry together. I am sure they had heard it before, but there seemed to be a new determination to implement this basic Biblical principle. Thus, we entered into the ministry together, the people and I, and five of the most wonderful years of my life were spent there. That situation was duplicated in the next two churches. I soon learned that the word *fellowship* meant more than doughnuts and coffee or a typical Baptist potluck; fellowship was a joint participation of pastor and people. As a young man in Hazel Park, Michigan, I had learned the phrase "organized obedience" as it applied to a church visitation program. Our churches in the Pacific Northwest learned that concept well, and organized obedience occurred every Monday night as God's people gathered together to reach the lost for Christ. In our last church, Temple Baptist of Tacoma, we saw over one hundred people gather every Monday night for our visitation outreach program. For thirteen years (part of which time I was the president of Northwest Baptist Seminary), the people of God stood with me in the program and it was a delightful experience. We were pulling the wagon together!

A Revival of Plurality

We live in a day when a great deal is said about authority. It is sad but true that the reason for much confusion in the church with regard to leadership is the influx of Christian education specialists who have come up with innovations in church organization and practice. While there are certainly exceptions to this rule, if we believe and practice everything these specialists say, we will have "organized experimental confusion."

Whenever I read of a church trying to "go it alone" without pastoral leadership, a warning bell goes off in my mind. The fact is, a church cannot survive without strong leadership, generally by a pastor.

One of the leading proponents of leadership by several elder-pastors in the church is Gene Getz. His book *Sharpening the Focus of the Church* has resulted in a revival of plurality of leadership. "A final observation regarding leadership in the New Testament church is that we always see a plurality of leadership. There is no reference to the appointment of 'one' elder or 'one' deacon for any given church. Obviously, no one individual was ever asked to serve alone."[1] That book was written in 1974. Getz, who still, as far as we know, believes in multiple elders, has tempered his view regarding the pastor and his leadership role.

In a 1981 issue of *Leadership* magazine (a publication I recommend), he debates Larry Richards in an article entitled "A Biblical Style of Leadership." The introduction to the article, after stating that Getz had decided to put what he had been teaching into action, adds: "The small group he began blossomed into a home church, which has expanded into four congregations and eight branch churches. Through all that expansion, and now in his role as director of the Dallas Center for Church Renewal, Getz's ideas about how to run a church have modified as he has wrestled with the problems of growth."[2] In the middle of the debate Getz says:

> I think the strongest point of your book, Larry, is when you tell pastors not to let people fixate on you, not to let them see you, the pastor, as a substitute for Christ as the head of the church. You had to work like crazy to keep that from happen-

ing. We've seen nine churches come into exis-
tence around Dallas in eight years; actually, we
have four churches that met in one building and
we've helped start, directly and indirectly,
eight branches. All of them owe their success to
the strength of the Holy Spirit working through
a strong group of elders; but there has also been a
strong pastor/leader, the man in the pulpit, the
one who sets the tone for the ministry. What up-
sets many people is the claim by some that certain successful churches don't have such a
leader. I maintain they all do. He may be "laid
back" in style, but he still leads. I think that's the
reason for some reactions to your book, Larry.[3]

A more recent issue of *Leadership* includes an interview with Gene Getz under the title "Sharpening the
Pastor's Focus." The question is asked, "How has your
leadership style changed since your early days in the
First Fellowship Bible Church?" Getz answers:

I think I've gained more self-awareness—
more self-honesty, if I may coin that word. If you
had asked me ten years ago, "What makes this
church work?" I would have said, "Humanly
speaking, it's our multiple leadership, primarily the elders."
Today I'd answer that question by saying, "Our
elders are key but I'm the key to helping the elders function." I don't mean to sound egotistical,
but I'm more aware of the role I have to play behind the scenes—communicating, motivat-
ing, phoning every elder who misses a meeting
to fill him in on what happened. My style is the
same as before—laid back but working like cra-
zy. The difference is I'm willing to admit I'm
leading. In the early days I've overreacted to authoritarian leadership styles—which I still

think are unfortunate—but I've always led. Now I feel I'm more honest with myself and others about the importance of a strong leader, particularly in a growing church, and yet also developing a strong multiple leadership that does lead as a team.[4]

The reason we have gone to such lengths in dealing with this matter is because so many Baptist churches have gone to Getz's original book and used it as a premise to "play down" the pastor's role. As a Baptist I would state that while we may not agree with Getz's terminology of "multiple elders" we would certainly agree that the church can and should have multiple leadership. But there must be a "quarterback," someone who is not the whole team but a leader on the team. The real problem seems to arise when we move into one of two extremes. One extreme is the authoritarian leader who always has the last word and cannot be wrong, with deacons who nod at the proper time. The other extreme is a leadership based on confusion, with all the "equals" trying to decide what to do, resulting in the stagnation of the local body.

Another person who stood out in that period of church renewal and innovative church leadership was David Mains, who wrote the book *Full Circle* and whose church was a "success." He states:

> Soon I was flying around the country to lead seminars on what made Circle Church work. With Larry Richards and Clyde Hoeldtke, I helped to found Step 2, a national organization designed to stimulate meaningful church renewal. About a dozen times a year I spoke to pastors and denominational heads on the principles that fueled the activities at Circle.[5]

Mains then states that his church failed. In an article in *Leadership* in 1980 entitled "My Greatest Ministry

Mistakes" he states his number three mistake simply: "In encouraging the gifts of the congregation, I minimized my leadership role."[6] He continues:

> I believe this problem of minimizing the pastor's leadership is a disease spreading wildly through evangelical churches. Fifteen years ago the opposite problem existed: authoritarian leadership. But when the laity began emerging with a strong excitement about the faith, attention was so focused away from the pastor that his function was perceived to be almost unneeded. Seminaries began teaching the pastor's role as "enabling the congregation," without balancing emphasis on being a spokesman for God and leading by exhorting. Awakening of the laity is a beautiful thing; a pulsing, vital sign in the history of the church. But I believe in the Old Testament symbol of the mantle; the cloak signifying that God has set aside a leader for certain strengths and skills. Jesus wore the mantle in a beautiful way. Although he was a servant, he also carried authority and no one questioned who the leader was. If you push servant leadership too far you can turn the leader into a doormat and destroy him. Only if a people recognize that a leader holds tremendous invested dignity will they respect him and treat him as a leader. As I read the history of the church, without strong leaders even outbreaks of church renewal quickly fizzle. I would express the balance this way: leadership describes the office: servanthood describes the style of exercising that office.[7]

The conclusions to this chapter are obvious. Is the church a "one man show"? No indeed. The pastor is not to be pulling the wagon, with the congregation looking on.

That is not a Biblical procedure. Rather, the pastor is a gift to the church. Although not the single authority, he certainly is a shepherd seeking to give direction to the flock and feed the flock. As the church grows there may be a need for another pastor to help, but there must be a senior pastor. There must be a quarterback.

Balance! That is the answer. The church needs it. We are so prone to grab a new concept, even one that is totally unbiblical although loaded with good and sincere intentions, and run with it, such as the plurality of elders. Or we find ourselves reacting to an unpleasant situation, such as an authoritarian pastor. On one occasion, as a dear lady in the church was praying she got her tongue twisted. She meant to say, "God bless our *loving shepherd*" but embarrassingly she slipped out with "God bless our *shoving leopard.*" There is a chance that her slip was more prophetic than pathetic. We need more loving shepherds. But, to continue our "animal analogy," we dare not leave the pastors out there, like those poor mules, pulling the wagon alone.

End Notes

[1] Gene Getz, *Sharpening the Focus of the Church* (Chicago: Moody Press, 1974), p. 110.

[2] "A Biblical Style of Leadership," *Leadership* (Spring, 1981), p. 68.

[3] Ibid., p. 77.

[4] "Sharpening the Pastor's Focus," *Leadership* (Summer 1985),   pp. 13-14.

[5] David Mains, "My Greatest Ministry Mistakes,"*Leadership* (Spring 1980), p. 15.

[6] Ibid.

[7] Ibid.

CHAPTER EIGHT
Laymen in Action

It cannot be overemphasized that men and women in the church are a dynamic part of the church and its ministry. The layman is not a second-class citizen. We state this again because in our discussion of the layman-pastor relationship it may appear that the sole function of the layperson lies in being a "Santa's elf" to the pastor. The layperson must not be considered inferior to the pastor or other members of the staff but in step and in harmony with them. We are not featuring solos here but the complete orchestra. True, we have been talking a lot about the job of the pastor's "conducting" and this is certainly an important part, but what good is the conductor if there is no orchestra?

But the Pastor Prefers a Solo Role

Before we get into the specifics of the orchestral arrangement, let's face what is often a real problem in the church, namely, the pastor who does not have a team concept or who does not feel that the layman's ministry is more than an appendage to the main business of pastoring. How do we cope with this condition, especially since the pastor is in the place of leadership?

We urge the layperson to be patient, to try to understand the problem and to be used of the Holy Spirit to help solve it. Some pastors feel that a strong layman involvement in the church may threaten their position, and there are cases in which that very thing has happened. I remember a situation in which a layman suggested to the pastor that a more Biblical concept was the formation of a board of elders to assist the pastor in the work. The pastor, feeling that this was a worthwhile suggestion, went along with it. As soon as the change was made, however, the layman announced that the pastor, as the leader of the group, was no longer needed. What the pastor had initially accepted as a step to help him was really designed to cut off his ministry. His reaction was one of hurt and betrayal. It is my conviction that we need to be more occupied with the function of gifts rather than the pecking orders of position. The recognition that a pastor is to lead the flock is important; the recognition by the pastor of the body's total involvement in the church's function is equally important. However, we must also recognize that situations such as we just mentioned have left many pastors wary of voluntary layman involvement in the work of the ministry.

Another reason to be patient is that often it is young pastors who tend to feel threatened, especially when they are trying to assume respect for their leadership. Do not fault them for this; they are learning. It takes a while to understand that some of the laymen have forgotten more than the pastor might know on a given subject, and to learn that he should capitalize on the availability of service, not oppose it. If he has been taught that he is to step in and take control and have a "back door revival" when anyone disagrees with him, the problem goes back to his teachers. When he assumes a "shoving leopard" rather than a "loving shepherd" approach, the church will be on the verge of an explosion. However, the layman can help defuse the situation with prayer, patience and a readiness to see great potential in the pastor. In my observation of various churches, I have found that this problem of a threatened pastor—resulting in a show of muscle to compensate for it—is the source of a great many problems and church splits. Thank God for Spirit-filled laymen who demonstrate their maturity in their patience and longsuffering in such situations. I am so grateful for the laymen (many of whom were old enough to be my father or grandfather) who helped me in the early days of my ministry. While I cannot remember ever having a serious altercation or anything resembling a church split, I am sure that this was partly due to loving, concerned laymen who saw a young man trying hard to be a good pastor, and who were willing to serve *with him* to the glory of the Lord we all loved.

Dimensions of the Layman's Service

As a pastor moves along in his ministry, he becomes more aware of the importance of the "orchestral" type of ministry rather than his "solo" work. In other words, he comes to realize he can be more effective in his preaching and teaching ministry when each member of the local body is functioning at his/her full capacity. Rather than diminishing the pastor's ministry, such functioning actually enhances it. There is time for him to give himself more fully to the ministry of the Word—that to which he has been called.

1. Laymen to Laymen

An important function of the body is in its internal ministry, that is, the body ministering to the body as Paul exhorts in Galatians 6:2, "Bear ye one another's burdens," and earlier in Galatians 5:13, "For, brethren, ye have been called unto liberty; only use not liberty for an occasion to the flesh, but by love *serve one another.*" Again, "We then that are strong ought to bear the infirmities of the weak, and not to please ourselves" (Rom. 15:1). We are told to "... warn them that are unruly, comfort the feebleminded, support the weak, be patient toward all men" (1 Thess. 5:14). The principle of the body ministering to the body is stamped on almost every epistle of the New Testament. Remember, most of these books were not written to individuals but to churches. Members of the church caring, helping, blessing each other reflect a happy, healthy church. Of course the pastor's assistance in this ministry, as a shepherd, should not be overlooked. Having a shepherd's eye, ready to recognize the needs of the flock, he is often better able for him to encourage one member of the flock to help another. For example, a woman may have had a miscarriage. The pastor and his wife could encourage another who had a similar situation to be an encouragement to that hurting member of the body. A person has lost his job; the pastor knows that directing someone to him who also lost his job might do more good than anything the pastor might say or do. Other problems such as alcoholism, or teenage runaways, might be times when that extra support from other sympathetic members of the body would be a great encouragement.

Sometimes this function of the layman with his pastor can take on a more official, organized capacity. For example, some churches have a deacon-caring program in which the congregation is divided up into flocks with a deacon caring for each flock.

There are other areas where laymen can minister to laymen, including retreats, special prayer breakfasts and adult Sunday School classes.

2. Laymen and the World Out There

Naturally, there is more to the function of the church than ministering to itself. One reason for mutual ministry is to develop the spiritual health and strength necessary to fulfill the Great Commission. In every church I have pastored, there has been a strong visitation program in which the church reached out to the community in evangelism. I believe that the growth of Temple Baptist Church in Tacoma, for example, was due to their participation in putting New Testament principles of evangelism into action.

Equipped to Do the Job

In his fine book, *Foundations for Purposeful Church Administration,* Alvin J. Lindgren states:

> If the church is to become in fact a people of God, a community through whom the love of God is to be made known to man in a redemptive way, it is obvious that lay participation in the life and work of the church must be widespread. Only a church in which laymen assume major responsibility for carrying the load can be adequate to today's demands. When Paul Maves says that every pastor should see himself as a dean of a theological seminary, he means that the pastor must train the members of the Christian community for their mission. They will need training as Christian educators, evangelists, shepherds, stewards, youth workers, missionaries, social concerns workers, and as lay ministers of other kinds as well. It is the whole church that has a ministry to perform, and laymen need to be equipped for it.[1]

Earlier I mentioned the Biblical injunction that the pastor is to equip the saints for the work of the ministry (Eph. 4:11, 12). I also mentioned earlier our churches' six-week training sessions for "organized obedience"— our visitation programs. (A rather detailed presentation is made of this program in my book, *The Pastor, His Life and Work,* published by Regular Baptist Press.) Through such sessions I have found that, given the proper challenge and training (equipping), laypeople are more than willing to do their part. They are generally grateful and appreciative when the pastor takes time to show them how to lead others to Christ and leads them and instructs them in Christian service. Then there are the areas where the pastor is instructed by the laymen. I am thinking, for example, of a group of laymen and their pastor who took a few weeks off to go to South America where they helped put up a church building. In that case, the laymen were teaching their pastor about construction.

I remember in one pastorate a banker and his wife expressed to me their desire to leave their work and be involved in a short-term stint on the mission field, helping in the area of finance. What a blessing it was to be partners with them as our church supported them in this ministry. It was a prime example of joint participation—of God's people doing God's work together. The church, as someone has put it, was a "launching pad" from which the laymen were propelled to service, a vital part of the total ministry of the church.

What a marvelous picture we have here: the pastor and the laymen, hand in hand, doing the will of God together. Yes, they are shepherd and flock, pastor and people, but they are at the same time Christian and Christian, servant and servant—they are a team, marching in step with the Lord and having the same heartbeat.

End Note
[1] Alvin J. Lindgren, *Foundations for Purposeful Church Administration* (Nashville: Abingdon Press, 1965), p. 188.

CHAPTER NINE
Let's Talk about Money Matters

Many times a pastor may want to sit down with his people and unburden his heart regarding matters of money—but he usually doesn't. Actually, if it were not for the fact that I am no longer in the pastorate, I would probably eliminate this chapter. But we need to face these issues head-on.

A Sensitive Issue

Yes, money is a sensitive issue, which is why there is more thought than talk about it. However, we must not feel that money is constantly on the mind of the pastor. After all, he has been called of God and senses this call deeply. Generally he feels good about being in the ministry and is grateful to God for the privilege of serving in this way. Also, he probably never expected to be paid comparable to others in the secular world with similar background and education. A recent survey by *Leadership* magazine reports, "Six out of ten ministers do not feel they are, or ever have been, financially deprived, mistreated or exploited by a ministry situation."[1] Of the 40 percent who said they had been exploited, half no longer feel that way. The only negative experience was their first church. When a pastor preaches that God will take care of us and supply all our needs, he generally applies this principle to his own life. Probably the most difficult time for a pastor will be that first year. Why? One reason could be that he has higher expectations than he should.

This could be the reason why there is so much ministerial burnout. One study shows 15 percent of seminary graduates don't survive their first pastorate, and it suggests that one of the factors is inadequate compensation.

If a pastor is not compensated enough he usually does not talk about it. He may feel that it is beneath his position to discuss it, and he certainly does not want to be considered a hireling. Often he will get a second job, especially if the church is small and simply cannot pay the pastor more than they are paying. A second possibility of supplemental income is the pastor's wife going to work. Studies show that almost one half of pastors' wives work outside the home (although this is not always due to necessity; some wives simply prefer to work). A third way of handling insufficient income is that, in some cases, the pastor might move on to another work where his basic needs will be provided. While hopefully this will not be the major reason for moving, it could very well enter the picture if the pastor feels that he is not adequately providing for his family.

A Neglected Area of Consideration

Since the pastor's compensation is such an important area, why is it not being met head-on in the church? There are several reasons.

1. The pastor does not make it an issue, as we have already discussed.

2. The congregation feels they are being cared for. In other words, they assume that since their needs are being met, the pastor's are too.

3. It is easy to put off. If a particular year is hard-pressed financially, it is easy to delay solving the problem of the pastor's income "until next year."

4. There is no standing committee to deal with this subject yearly. Manfred Holck, Jr., in *Leadership,* suggests a standing committee of five to seven persons to re-

view the salary annually. Their selection is determined by 1. influence in congregation decision making, 2. positive attitudes about the ministry in general and the pastor in particular, 3. a working knowledge of clergy compensation, 4. awareness of the church budget, its limitations, and its support from the membership, 5. an unwavering in commitment to the cause of the Gospel and to fair, equitable treatment of all persons, including their financial concerns.[2]

In a survey, 62 percent of the lay leaders questioned thought it was possible to remedy any inequity between pastor and people. Sixty-five percent of the underpaid pastors agreed. But, this being so, the subject of the pastor's pay still is not being dealt with. It is simply not an agenda item, especially if the church has no yearly budget. In other words, it is just neglected.

What Is Included in the Salary?

The congregation generally understands what is included in the pastor's salary (that is, the actual amount the pastor gets per week or month): his housing allowance, if there is no parsonage, and utility allowances; any hospitalization or other insurance and any pension or savings plan. Also a consideration, although not salary in the full sense of the word, would be a car allowance, book allowance, and any continuing education compensation for seminars, further schooling, tapes, etc. Some churches have a fund for the pastor's use in entertaining such guests as new prospects and missionaries at home or in restaurants.

Determining the Salary

In an excellent survey, both lay leaders and ministers expressed what factors should determine ministerial compensation. Using a rating scale of 1–not important to 10–very important, the survey showed the following results:

Clergy Values	Evaluation Factors	Laity Values
10	Amount of responsibility	10
9	Ability to relate to wide range of problems	9
8	Strengths of pulpit ministry	8
7	Ministry results	8
6	Length of service	4
5	Educational credentials	5
5	Median income of congregation	5
4	Size of congregation	6
4	Size of budget	7
3	Expertise in specialized ministry	4
2	Size of staff	3
2	Compensation of fellow clergy in denomination	3
1	Age	1[3]

A study of this survey will show that the conclusions of the pastor and the layman are rather similar except in two areas. The budget size is not as important to the pastor as it is to the layman. The layman probably thinks the pastor should put more emphasis on money, which would result in his getting more. The pastor is probably more people-minded. The other area in which they differ is length of service, which seems to mean more to the pastor than to the layman. Although a pastor may have a total of ten years in the ministry, perhaps he has spent just one of those ten years in the present church, where he is still perceived to be new, and combined tenure is not always considered.

Frequent Mistakes with Respect to the Pastor and His Salary

Several "mistakes" or misapprehensions are generally prevalent when the subject of the pastor's salary is being considered. Let's look at them.

1. This pastor is just beginning; we need not start him at the same salary as the preceding pastor."

This is a common observation. Just a little thought should clear it up. Has the new pastor been in the Lord's work for several years or is he just beginning? If this pastorate is not his first, then this observation is meaningless. Consideration should be focused more on the church's ability to pay commensurate with what the last pastor received—or more. It could be that the salary was not reviewed properly during the last pastorate; now is a good time to get it to where it should be.

2. "Our church isn't very large and we can't pay as well as we should."

This can be a problem, but be sure that it is a *real* problem. Sometimes with a readjustment of the budget and cutting in other places, the church can do what they *should* do.

Many churches have a formidable missionary budget and yet are not meeting their pastor's financial needs. Does this mean that the church should cut off some of its missionaries? Certainly not, but it does mean that before other budget increases are made, the church should do right by the pastor. When the church is responsible in this area of the pastor's salary, it can expect to be blessed of God and prosper.

3. "Every year we give the pastor a 5 percent raise; sometimes even 10 percent."

You are to be commended. But is this raise based on his service, or are you simply keeping up with inflation, which means that essentially he is making what he did before? Do not mistake my motive in asking this; as I said before, pastors generally are not after money. But we ought to call it what it is, and such honesty will benefit both pastor and the church.

4. "There are a lot of fringe benefits which, when totaled, show that he gets much more than it seems."

Excellent, and you are to be commended for thinking through ways and means of helping him. It is proper to consider hospitalization for the pastor and his family, a pension or savings plan, or a house in which to live as salary. But there are other things, such as a car allowance and other allowances that help him in the work of the church, which should not be considered a salary benefit.

5. "Our pastor has only two children. Also, his wife works part- time. So his needs are not as great as those of the pastor we had before."

This is the most subtle mistake of all. I find that often in Christian work (and Christian schools are the worst offenders) we give on the basis of need, not worth and ability. While we do not apply this in the workaday world (there we would call it socialism—"to each according to his need and from each according to his ability"), we are quick to find it to be proper in the church. The church cannot be expected to give beyond its ability, but when it is able to give, the pastor's salary should not be based upon need alone. Think this one through, and you will probably not want to apply this socialistic principle in the church.

Now, let's sum up this section by repeating that no man of God is in this work for the money. He has enough sense to know that if making money was his goal, he should have gone in a different occupational direction. But it is time that we looked at this subject fairly and squarely, and you will find that responsibility to your pastor in the area of his salary will ultimately benefit your church.

Where Should He Live

One survey indicated that 60 percent of all pastors and their families lived in a parsonage (or manse). Only 40 percent owned their own homes. However, I think in ten years we will find this reversed. Let's look at the advantages of both.

Advantages of Living in a Parsonage

Here are some of the most obvious advantages of the church owning a parsonage: there is no worry on the part of the pastor and his family with the upkeep; there is not the problem of selling a house when he feels led of the Lord to move (nor is it an issue in whether or not to move, as it might be if he had a great deal invested in a house and tended to stay when he should be thinking otherwise). From the vantage point of the church, the parsonage is included in the worth of the church holdings and could increase in value. Also, if the church decided to encourage the pastor to buy a house, they could have a white elephant on their hands with the old parsonage. They would have to decide what to do with the house, how it could be used. That latter problem is not as great as it seems when you remember that missionaries on furlough often need a place to stay. A guest home is not only desirable but becomes almost mandatory as the church grows.

Advantages of a Pastor Owning His Home

There are several advantages of a pastor owning his home. I have had it both ways, living in fine parsonages and later owning two homes. Frankly, every home was a delight. We were never given cause to complain about the places God gave us to live; they were more than adequate.

However, the equity we received in the last two homes was most encouraging, especially as we look to the future for retirement. The only savings many pastors will ever have is what they have in the homes they own. There is a hedge against inflation when a home is owned, as it is being paid off with inflated dollars and was bought at a lower price. I have known pastors who lived in parsonages all their lives and, when they retired, did not have enough saved to buy a home.

There is also a tax advantage to owning a home. When a church gives a housing allowance to buy a home, the allowance is not considered salary and is not subject to income tax. Also, the interest paid on a house is deductible (as is the case for every home buyer). So, in effect, there is a double deduction. For example, if a pastor's mortgage payment was five hundred dollars a month, he would not have to pay tax on that amount. And, if most of the payments, especially earlier in the purchase, were interest (let us say four fifths, or four hundred dollars), then there would be a nine hundred dollar tax benefit. If this seems strange, it is not. It is a legal deduction that is allowed for ministers, and it is another reason why it is wise for a pastor to buy his own home.

Another advantage is that the pastor and his family can buy according to their needs and exercise some choices in the kind of house they want. The church with a parsonage is forced to buy a rather large house, anticipating different sizes of families. But the pastor with a small family can choose the house which best meets his family's situation. For example, I have nine thousand volumes in my personal library. Finding a home anywhere that would be sturdy enough to house that size of library would be difficult, to say nothing of putting it in an "average" parsonage.

Of course there are some advantages to the church when the pastor buys his own home. First, they know that he is happy and has the kind of house that meets his needs. Second, they do not have the problem of keeping the parsonage in repair.

While there are advantages both ways, I would suggest that the church consider asking the pastor what he would prefer and try, if at all possible, to make arrangements accordingly.

End Notes
[1] Paul D. Robbins, Leadership, (Spring 1981), p. 36.

[2] Manfred Holck, Leadership, (Winter 1980), pp. 40–44.

[3] Paul D. Robbins, Leadership,(Spring 1981), p. 42.

CHAPTER TEN

Five Statements Every Pastor Is Reluctant to Make

No, you will not be surprised when you find out what the five statements are. You may have made them yourself. After all, the point of this chapter is that pastors are human too. They have inclinations and tendencies like the rest of us, it is just that we do not hear them express them as much. We have an image of what a pastor is like: he is a man of God and therefore he does not get discouraged or down. But let's look at these five statements and then respond to them. It could be that we will change our minds about a pastor's image.

I Am So Tired of Pushing Everything

There is a story about a successful pastor who had a secret that aroused everyone's curiosity. Every week, on a certain day, he left the community he served and went over a hill and through the woods to a secret place. He refused to discuss it with anyone. Actually, according to the story, that little secret almost did him in. People began to talk and speculate and, if he had not divulged where he went and what he did, a scandal could very easily have been started. At the prompting of the board of deacons he finally "confessed" his little weekly journey. He said that at a certain time every week he went over the hill and through the woods to a certain place along the railroad track. Every day at 3:10 in the afternoon the last train of the day would pass by. The pastor said: "I sit by the track, watch the train, and thank the Lord that there is at least one thing in this town that I don't have to push."

Of course the story is apocryphal, but the point is true. Many pastors have to push and push and push people to do things until there is no push left.

No, most of us do not want to admit it, but it is there for us to face. We must go back to the P.M. (Partners in the Ministry) principle again. When we all see ourselves as a vital part of the ministry, and further understand that the purpose of the pastor is not to do it all himself but to equip the saints to do "the work of the ministry," much of this "one-man-push-and-perform" syndrome seems to disappear.

I Really Want to Be Left Alone

Don't misunderstand this one. Generally the pastor is a people person, and it is inconsistent for a shepherd to avoid being around his flock. The point here is that most pastors want *some* privacy. It is necessary for their well-being; it is vital if they are going to be "charged" spiritually, and it is important for their homelife.

Yes, even the pastor has a right to feel that his privacy is being invaded. He is not supernatural; he needs time to relax, time to be alone to reflect on his ministry, time to be rejuvenated and time to renew his commitments to his family. Here are some areas to consider to assure the pastor of some breathing room.

1. Do not treat the parsonage as an extension of the church. If the parsonage is near the church, especially on the church grounds, it is often treated like an extension to the church. We have heard of congregation members frequently using parsonage bathrooms, mothers bringing in their babies to be changed and other activities which might be expected in a "wing of the church." "Af-

ter all," goes the argument, "it is our property, isn't it?" We once heard of a party who wanted to build a swimming pool on the parsonage grounds so the pastor and his family could relax and enjoy it together. In a church meeting there was a question as to whether the pool could be used during certain hours by the church members. The pastor, sensing a difficulty, suggested the idea of a pool be dropped. That was the end of the swimming pool. It would help tremendously if the parsonage could be considered a private dwelling place rather than church property.

2. Do not treat the pastor's children as though they live in a fish bowl. Why do so many p.k.'s (preacher's kids) turn out the way they do? Someone has suggested that it is because they are always around d.k.'s (deacon's kids)! Seriously, it is a formidable challenge to raise children with the eyes of the congregation following their every move. A special effort should be made to view them the same way as the other children in the congregation.

3. There are too many instances of a pastor's wife becoming resentful and even bitter at the many demands placed on her husband, even to the extent that she feels she is considerably low on the list of his priorities. This is regrettable, but it is also preventable. To be sure, part of the blame is the pastor's for allowing it to happen. But the church is not without some of the blame. A board that insists that the pastor take some time off is a wise board. A board and church that are aware of the needs of the pastor's family and spend time trying to meet those needs are to be commended. A church that does not feel offended when the pastor insists on a private life, and does not feel he is neglecting his job if he gets away occasionally, is a church that is to be congratulated for its wisdom and foresight. A pastor and family that is physically, mentally and spiritually healthy is a vital asset to any church. It is important to help protect their privacy.

I'm Not Making It on My Salary

We have already dwelt on this subject, but it behooves us to realize, again, just how difficult it is to say, "I'm not making it on my salary." Often, congregations do not understand that the pastor and his family may have financial demands not generally found in the average home. For instance, he probably wears a suit every day, he entertains often, and he is expected to be constantly preparing new messages, necessitating a growing library.

We are not pleading that the pastor be treated like a king. We are simply asking that the church be sensitive to his needs. Most churches will do all they can; the problem, often, is just knowing that a problem exists. It takes only a few in the congregation taking the lead to make a difference.

I Have a Spiritual Need

We need to keep in mind that pastors have spiritual needs too. Without going into the need of pastors being more transparent and more open about themselves, it should be sufficient to admit that they are human and in constant need of prayer. Could the problem be that we have created such a gap between pastor and people that he cannot share his heart needs? Perhaps; but in the same way that a doctor does not share his physical hurts with his patient, the pastor may feel that to share his own needs might lessen the effectiveness of his help. Again, the pros and cons of how this type of situation should be handled have been debated. But the fact is, this is the way it is; so rather than fault him, let's help him by surrounding him with prayer and understanding.

My Work Seems to Be Finished Here

Perhaps the hardest statement of all is "My work seems to be finished here," especially if the pastor has had a successful ministry. He knows that his leaving will cause much hurt and even some misunderstanding. But once this statement is made, the congregation needs to be willing to accept it as from the Lord. Let me tell you the sensation every pastor feels when he decides to move to another work: he feels alone, and he feels that the relationship is changed between him and his people. I have warned young seminarians about this and told them that once they decided to move on, even though the people loved and respected them, there would be an immediate distantness in the relationship. I would very much like for members of congregations reading this to prove me wrong. If a loving, caring, understanding spirit could exist in the congregation after this decision is made, it would be a great blessing. I am not suggesting that the spirit usually is cruel or hostile, but there is often a withdrawing which is both noticeable and hurtful.

CHAPTER ELEVEN

Little Areas, Big Results

When we make an investment we expect to get some return on it. While we generally do not think of a pastor as an investment, in a sense he is just that. The more we put into areas that will enhance his ministry, the more return will be accrued by the church. On the surface this sounds a little selfish, but we are not talking about personal benefit; we are talking about the benefit to the local church and the cause of Christ. We are simply stating that we often receive commensurate to what we give. Some simple, "down to earth" investments will result in some big, blessed benefits.

The Pastor and His Books
I have long felt that if a church would encourage the pastor in his acquiring of books they would be better off. But the fact is, many pastors canot afford books. Obviously there are some they will buy whether they can afford them or not, but when a pastor is struggling to meet his regular bills and keep food on the table, he is not likely to be buying many books.

Why not start a book fund for the pastor from which he can purchase books that will help him in his preaching and teaching? A fund of just ten dollars a month would be a good start. Even twenty-five dollars a month would come to only three hundred dollars a year, within the budget of even the smallest church. The books would become the property of the pastor; but the church would reap the benefit.

A Pension for the Parson?

What do pastors do when they retire? Many continue to preach and minister in some area. It's in their blood! But another question might be, *How,* financially, do they do it? Frankly, thousands of pastors face this problem. And the problem has often been created because of something they have done right! Many pastors are independent enough not to belong to denominations that compromise in their stand. They have refused such affiliation because such yielding to the demands of others was too high a price to pay, even if it meant some degree of financial hardship when they retired. On the other hand, some pastors would have left such denominations, but the promise of a healthy pension was a factor in their failing to make a clean break. Should a pastor be worse off financially because of his convictions? Ask him and he will tell you that in the long run he is not worse off and he would do it again. But what an encouragement it would be if his congregation stood with him and helped him in his plans for retirement. What a help it would be if the church withdrew, for instance, 5 percent of his salary every month and matched it with another 5 percent for his retirement. Over twenty years this would be a considerable amount if placed in some type of mutual plan or some pension plan. (There are many insurance plans available for pastors.) Of course, if he moved on he would be able to take that amount with him, and over the years it would build up. Think about it. This is one of those areas that will rarely be discussed if we leave it up to the pastor.

The Preacher's Chariot

With the pastor's many responsibilities, his car is important to him. Frequently, the church pays for his mileage or, better still, they may supply a new car for him every two or three years. Most of his driving will be for the benefit of the church. Unlike a job that requires only eight hours, his is ongoing and involves twenty-four hours a day.

He's Good, but He Can Be Better

As a college and seminary president, I have learned the importance of making sure that our administrators and management people keep up on new developments in their fields. We spend thousands of dollars every year to send various administrators "back to school" in seminars designed to improve their effectiveness to the institution. The same is true with our faculty—sabbaticals are offered after several years of teaching. Frankly, I have become more aware of the necessity of continuing education and ways and means of implementing it since I have been in the field of education. But isn't it just as important for the pastor to keep up with new methods in church administration and growth and in counseling skills? And isn't it important for him to remain fresh in his constant preparation of sermons? Aren't we all the beneficiaries of his growing in these areas?

If the average church would invest in the ongoing education and training of the pastor, it would no longer remain average. Here are some areas where a few dollars a month could make the difference between a fresh, alert, helpful pastor and one that is jaded, tired and discouraged.

1. Send the pastor and his wife to a Bible conference.

Every year in February, hundreds of people come to the annual Bible conference in Grand Rapids, Michigan, and every year I write a letter to hundreds of churches urging each one to send the pastor and his wife. Many of them do just that. And the fact that they do it year after year must mean that they feel it rejuvenates, restores and refreshes them both. The church is better for it also. There are several Bible conferences in various parts of the country, so take the initiative and send them to at least one every year.

2. Encourage the pastor to attend seminars.

There is a joke going around that there are so many seminars, we will soon need a seminar on seminars. However, while it is true that anything good can be overdone, it is just as true that seminars in such areas as counseling, church growth and church finance will broaden the scope and vision of the pastor. Have you noticed that pastors of growing, going, aggressive churches have frequently had some background in that kind of church? They have seen how a successful church is developed, they have experienced it in action—they have been part of its success. On the other hand, some pastors in small, dying churches give the impression that they will never be anything else. Often this kind of situation remains the same because the pastor has never known anything but a small work that creeps and crawls along. We are not suggesting that it is wrong to be small (if there is no potential for growth), nor is it spiritual to be big. But we are suggesting that it is right to be healthy and dynamic, with vigorous strides being made regularly. Often the pastor lacks exposure to these possibilities and potentials, but he can gain exposure through seminars that give him "hands-on experience" with a pastor experienced in church growth.

3. Encourage the pastor to expand his formal education.

Many seminaries have special programs designed to help the "veteran" pastor. For example, the Grand Rapids Baptist Seminary offers advanced degrees in a course in which pastors can do the reading and instruction away from the seminary campus, as long as they spend several weeks every summer on the campus. This is not an "easy degree," and many of the courses require several years in the ministry. Another area is the doctorate of ministries program designed for the pastor who has his master of divinity degree and has been in service for a number of years.

The church will find a great return on its investment of encouraging the pastor to "get away" for the training and even helping with the cost.

There is really no end to the possibilities in this area of self-improvement. A visit to the Holy Land, for example, will help make the Bible live for both the pastor and those to whom he ministers. A visit to the mission fields of missionaries supported by your church will literally help turn around the missionary thrust of the church.

Yes, some of these things are "pluses" for the pastor; but they are also pluses for the congregation. A fundamental congregation with the Lord's work and the Lord's servants at heart will find real joy in helping in the ways suggested. "Give, and it shall be given unto you . . ." (Luke 6:38).

CHAPTER TWELVE
Trouble with the Little Foxes

In the Song of Solomon we read, "Take us the foxes, the little foxes, that spoil the vines: for our vines have tender grapes" (Song of Sol. 2:15). Every pastor has a list of "little foxes," little irritants that disrupt the church service. It is almost embarrassing to mention them because each one, when considered alone, seems so innocent and unimportant. But they still do harm, and getting some of these irritants "off the pastor's chest" might prove helpful. As we examine the foxes, you might find yourself saying, "I didn't know it mattered that much to the pastor or I would have acted before now."

Whispering
Unless you have been involved in public speaking or preaching, you have no idea of the impact the fox we call "whispering" can have on the message. Even for a veteran speaker, it can be tough. It may be a couple of adults discussing something serious, but it can have devastating results. Every pastor wishes to have liberty when he preaches, that is, a "freedom" when words just seem to flow, and thoughts are there when he needs them, and there is a sense of God's presence and power. Sometimes this freedom is missing because of lack of preparation or sin in his life. Sometimes the evident power of the satanic world oppresses him. But he can also be hindered by a conversation in the pew—either whispered or in pass-

ing notes. (Think of it: we have put the work of the satanic world next to whispering as the cause of interruption!) Whether it is as a roaring lion or a little fox of a gentle whisper invading the service, Satan can hinder the work of the Spirit through the pastor.

The Kid in Front

How many times have you watched a little child move around in the pew in front of you? He is cute and he knows it, and he is encouraged by your wink or smile or subtle motion. Suddenly that whole section of the auditorium is involved in the little circus. Meanwhile, standing up front is God's messenger, with God's holy Word in his hand, praying as he preaches that the "little fox" in that area of the sanctuary will settle down.

Well-Read Worshipers

Another fox reads during the service! That's right, when anything is available to read, it will be read by this studious vixen. Is there a bulletin available? How about Sunday School papers or a book from the church library? He will even read detailed notes in his Bible. Whenever there is a lack of attention, however quiet and "undisturbing" it might be to those around, believe me, the pastor is aware of it. He is struggling and even hurting about it up there behind that sacred desk.

Church Is for Ushers Too

Another fox-like episode takes place in the back of the church, often in the foyer. The ushers have greeted the people and have taken the offering, but they are still standing in the back. They may be counting the money, counting the people, counting their blessings or counting the minutes before the pastor finishes—but they are also spoiling the "tender grapes." Sometimes they can be heard or seen in the back, and their absence from their place beside their wives is always felt. Don't *they* need the message? Don't *they* care about this important part of the service? The pastor knows he should correct the situation, but he probably will say little since the ushers are often leaders and the subject is sensitive. Besides, they probably do not know the damage that is being done to the fruit. And this situation is such a *little* fox. . . .

Foxes that Tell Time

Have you noticed that the congregation is more time conscious than any other group in the world? When the pastor preaches over thirty minutes, they grow restless. Some turn their heads to see the clock. Others ever so carefully turn their arms to see their wristwatches. The bolder ones even hold their watches to their ears to ascertain if they are ticking. No matter that they could sit in front of a TV for three hours or, after the service is over, spend lots of time fellowshiping (the latter being much more healthful and helpful than the former).

I have heard of congregations bringing up the time matter during a service, and as a pastor I can remember the board mentioning—ever so gently—that a forty minute message could be a little too much.

Tell Me Something I Haven't Heard

The last little fox "tunes out" the pastor even when he is looking right at the pastor. Every pastor knows of people in the congregation who simply do not listen. They are there—yet they are not. To them the service is simply a ritual, and they are there only in body.

The purpose of this little chapter is not to get these annoying situations off my chest. I am no longer a pastor. But I do know that these foxes exist, and who better to discuss them with than the spiritual layman who does not want anything to hinder the Lord's work. Let's look at ways of dealing with the foxes—once and for all.

First, instead of whispering or talking during the message, try being in an attitude of prayer for the pastor as he preaches God's Word. Determine that anything important to say now can be said later, but for now you have come to listen to God as He speaks to you through His holy Word.

Second, when there is a distraction in the congregation, try to be a part of solving it rather than part of the problem. For example, if a child is the cause, you could gently remind the parents about the nursery or junior church. Also, careful attention to the music or speaker in spite of distraction shows concern, discipline and polite holiness.

Third, set aside some time during the Lord's Day to read the bulletin, the Sunday School papers and any other distracting material. But during the message, "set your affection (mind)" on heavenly things and try to get the message God has for you.

Fourth, generally when we like (or love) something, time passes before we know it. To be too time conscious shows a spiritual problem. It might help to work on preparing your heart before the service and applying the message to your own life. To be "lost" in the vineyard—gathering fruit for your own soul—will result in being less time conscious and more God conscious.

Fifth, if, as an usher, you are also a church leader, remember that all eyes are on you. You are more responsible than the person who is not a leader. A leader leads and sets examples. A leader is seen, observed and emulated. Try not to think of yourself as one who is the exception to the normal rules, but as one who should exemplify them in your conduct. When your service is rendered let it be done humbly and faithfully, and then find your place with the rest of the congregation. If you have business to care for, do it after the service. True, such matters as counting the offering money or meeting with the trustees about building matters are important. But they are means to the end, and the end is the service itself. See yourself as part of God's people meeting *together* for mutual encouragement and strength as you fellowship and are blessed and instructed by the Word.

Finally, to the person who is in the service in body only, I say we need to ask the Lord to help us approach each service with a prayerful, caring attitude. Whenever we approach the holy as if it were mundane, whenever we think of the sermon as a lecture rather than a personal message to us, we are on the losing end.

Yes, the foxes are little, but little things can make a big difference in a church service.

CHAPTER THIRTEEN

When Things Go Wrong

The Pastor Is Vulnerable

This is the part of the book I do not enjoy writing because it is about confrontation between the pastor and his people. Let us begin by saying, first of all, that the pastorate is at once one of the most precious and most precarious jobs in the world. It can be one of victory and satisfaction but also vulnerability. In other words, if the congregation does not like what the pastor is saying—about sin in the church, for instance—they may show him the door. On the other hand, if the sin is not resolved, the pastor may leave voluntarily, purely out of conviction. So it is not always a matter of doing right and staying or doing wrong and leaving. We must be careful, as members of the board and members of the congregation, not to penalize the parson for the courage of his convictions. Remember, Paul was one of the most criticized of all, but the criticism did not mean that he was wrong. In fact, the critics were carnal Christians at Corinth. We need to recognize that carnality cannot stand holiness of life. It does not like to be put down or exposed. So let us determine that before we begin to criticize we will first examine our own hearts and lives and make sure that the problem, whatever it is, does not begin with us. The pastor is first of all a minister of God and is responsible to God. Granted, a holy man should be able to express himself without being a "human hammer" against the congregation, but wouldn't

107

we much rather have a man who deals with sin, even in a way considered by some as unkind, than a man who ignores sin?

The Beginning of a Problem

Let's assume that a disagreement has arisen between a member of the congregation and the pastor. First and foremost, a person who has a grievance should search his heart and pray, "See if there be any wicked way in me." Knowing ourselves is sometimes very difficult, but examining our motives is very important. Why does the member feel the way he does about the pastor? Could it be a matter of the pastor's style? Has the member considered the pastor's viewpoint, given the pastor's present set of circumstances? Would the member be better off to swallow his pride, knowing that it was this area of pride that precipitated the feeling? Is the disagreement a matter of taste and preference or a difference in methodology rather than moral principle? These are important considerations. It could be that, after much prayer, the matter should be dropped. If harsh words have been exchanged, it might be necessary to settle the matter one-on-one with the pastor.

Have you noticed that a great deal of church divisions and splits have begun with nit-picking? A small, insignificant matter chafes and galls, resulting in a louder voice and more determined mind and then explodes out of proportion, leaving confusion and often bitterness.

Be Scriptural in Your Complaint

Let's assume that the difference between the pastor and the layman is not minor. The layman needs to continue to pray and to personally consult the Scriptures, being sure that they are the basis for the difference. He should be careful not to go to another member and share his complaint.

The Scriptural order in an offense is to go first to the offender. It may be necessary, later, to take another person along to approach him again, and only if the matter cannot be resolved at that point should it become a matter for the church. This is spelled out clearly in Matthew 18:15-17.

When the layman does approach the pastor, he might simply state that he is approaching the pastor about something that is bothering him personally. The layman needs to assure the pastor that he loves him and that he loves the church, and that it is because he wants the truth, and wants to help everybody involved, that he is approaching the pastor. I believe that more often than not, with the help of the Lord and the desire to communicate, they can work out the difficulty with a dose of "Spirit-filled" longsuffering and patience. Thus a great many matters can be cleared up and heart-breaking circumstances avoided.

A Vote of Confidence

Often, when there are problems between a pastor and his congregation, the church will call for a vote of confidence to help determine whether he should stay. Sometimes such a vote is requested by the pastor himself. Personally, I cannot find this principle spelled out or even hinted at in Scripture. It frequently turns out to be a no-win situation for the pastor because the very fact that the vote is taken shows that there is no confidence, at least by some of the congregation. As a pastor, I always felt that if a church situation got to that point, a vote of confidence would not be necessary; I would take that attitude as an indication that I should move. (I am thankful I have never been subject to that kind of situation, due to the love and compassion of five wonderful congregations.)

If as a church you still feel that such a vote is useful, be careful in calling for it. It is not a credit to the church when the majority votes "no confidence" and the minority leaves to begin another church down the street. The testimonies of both congregations are affected.

Be Patient and Prayerful

Let me make a confession. I do feel that church splits are frequently precipitated by the pastor. If he has an unscriptural view of his position and insists that he is speaking ex cathedra on all subjects and therefore cannot be wrong, then he is the problem. But even in this set of circumstances the laymen need to do all they can to resolve the problem patiently and prayerfully. Remember, you are dealing with the Lord's church.

Guard against Secret Meetings

Secret meetings about a problem with the pastor are generally devastating, especially when they are disguised as prayer meetings. Getting together just to pray about such a situation more often than not ends up with a group sympathetic with each other's cause and a determination to take immediate action. It is very difficult to be objective in these matters. Only after the layman has prayed about the matter privately, then prayed with the pastor about it, should he even think of gathering with others to pray. And when they do gather, they should pray, not bray. They are to knock on Heaven's door, not on the pastor's head!

Preachers Protective Association

Are you convinced that I belong to the "Preachers Protective Association"? Do I seem biased in favor of the pastor? I am the first to admit that more often than not the pastor can be faulted for allowing a situation to go on. I have also discovered that the kind of pastor that causes problems in one church will frequently do so in every church he is in. So check this out before you call him. Questions about his temper, his reaction to pressure and criticism and his methods of handling problems are almost as important as his doctrinal positions. To find out later that he caused problems in other churches is not much comfort.

The Church Constitution

Usually the church constitution spells out the procedure for the dismissal of a pastor. Certainly it will be unfortunate—for both church and pastor— if it comes to this. Only after every other step has been prayerfully taken, and the parties involved have sought to work out their problems, should the church proceed to take action.

There are some cases, of course, of blatant sin, such as adultery or fornication. When such a case is properly verified, there needs to be prompt but careful and prayerful action on the part of the deacons and the church. Care should be given to help the persons involved in the sin as well as to preserve the purity of the church. While there are various views as to whether a person who has committed adultery should ever serve again in the ministry (it is my view that he should not), it is generally agreed that he should do so only after a long and adequate time period has passed, and only after the sin has been confessed and restitution made. There are no grounds for a pastor or the congregation to feel he should continue his ministry in that church.

Again, be sure that the method of dealing with this problem is in compassion and love. It would be in order for the church to meet for prayer and then deal with the situation in an official church meeting. While this is a difficult time, it can also be a time for learning. The purity and integrity of the church, as well as an attitude of love and compassion, are vital to the church and can meet in a wonderful way during a time of trauma and testing.

Going the Extra Mile

When a pastor leaves under difficult conditions, it is a good testimony to "go the extra mile" on his behalf so that, after it is all over, the church feels good about having done the right and fair thing. Consideration should be given to his personal needs and those of his family. Sometimes financial needs should be considered. When gross sin is involved, the sooner he leaves the better, for the church's sake; but, for his family's sake, meeting his financial needs for a month would not be out of order.

I hope you as a church will never have to go through this trauma. But if it does come, remember the Lord is able to help, sustain and see you through. Don't let such difficulties be a means of defeat but of learning, strengthening and leaning hard on Him.

CHAPTER FOURTEEN
Laymen I Have Known

After all is said and done, the bottom line in the function of the church is the actual practice of godliness, not simply the theory of it. This is also true with respect to service: it is not the "know-how" but the knowing and doing that counts. It is the application of the principles in this book that we are most interested in, not the discussion of them. To that end, let's look at some laymen who, in my opinion, exemplify some of these principles.

My Father

I think one of the hardest things I ever had to face was losing my father.

I was very young when my dad was saved, but I remember it well. Our family had not been going to church. While my parents were decent people, having been raised in Christian homes, they grew up without having trusted Christ. When my grandfather, on one occasion, asked my father where we were going to church, my father told him the truth: we were not going anywhere. My grandfather scolded Dad, and told him in firm language that the children ought to be taken to church by their parents. Dad responded and we attended the Tabernacle Baptist Church of Hazel Park, Michigan.

A dramatic change took place in our family when Mother and Dad were saved. From that time on I observed the godly example of my parents. My father was what I consider the ideal layman. When the doors of the church opened, Dad was there with his family. Was

there a visitation program? We were there. Special meetings? We were there. And always on time. Dad had a
thing about being late (anything less than thirty minutes
early was late to him). In the course of his ministry he was
the church treasurer, a trustee, a deacon and almost
everything else except a choir member. He was quiet, reserved and conservative, but he impacted my life by his
personal holiness and by being at home what he was in
the pew. When we did wrong, I knew it broke his heart.

I would like every layman to be like my father. I believe our churches would be stronger. My father was not
a preacher (he was self-conscious and nervous in front of
groups) but his life preached, and the sermon I received
is still being lived out in my life—a testimony to a great layman.

Julius Caesar Lowery

He was an old man when I was a young boy, and I
really didn't know him well. I only knew that there was a
very special pew where he sat in church, absorbing the
message, and that he was instrumental in leading
scores of people to the Lord. He was one of the laymen instrumental in starting a soul-winning "fishermen's
club," which eventually was the spark that caused Calvary Baptist Church of Hazel Park, Michigan, to be one of
the fastest-growing churches in the world. He put his
arm around me one day and said "Come on, kid, and I'll
show you how it's done." Thus I learned my first important lessons in organized obedience—the church visitation program—from an unimpressive-looking old man
who had a real heart for people.

A Layman Becomes a Pastor

Harold Sweetland had one of the most popular Bible
classes at Calvary Baptist Church, and no wonder. This
layman could wield the Sword of the Lord in a remark-

able fashion. He never had a formal education beyond high school, but he was an ardent reader and built a theological library that would more than match that of a trained Bible scholar. Thus it was not surprising to find him filling the pulpits of churches and ultimately accepting the call of a Baptist church in Wathams, Michigan. But, not content to simply pastor a church, he became one of the finest church planters I have ever known. He planted churches in Canada, Arizona, Washington, Idaho and Oregon, in most cases building them himself. He could swing a hammer and lead a working crew, as well as preach a message from the Word, all the time exhibiting a pastor's heart. Quite a combination. But in many ways he was always a layman, and a good one too.

Deacons, Deacons Everywhere

The five churches I pastored all had deacons who were very special to me. I cannot think of a time that we ever had a knock-down, drag-out confrontation. Some of them were my seniors, and some of them had forgotten more than I knew about many things. But they were loving, considerate, patient men who played a great part in my pastoral development.

A study of laymen can be just as interesting as a study of preachers. Just when you think you have seen them all, you find a unique "variety" whose mold has been thrown away. There is "Historical Harry" who is quick to say "We never did it that way before." On the other end of the spectrum is "New-Way Wally" who has just attended another seminar and discovered we are doing it all wrong. Then there is "What's-it-Cost Charlie" who watches the books with an eagle eye and is the first to exclaim that we can't afford it. Every trustee board has a "Got-a-Deal Neil" who can save a buck or two for the church if you will leave it to him. But they all make life that much more interesting, and we should love them for their weaknesses as well as their strengths.

Personalities aside, we must remember we are partners together with Christ. We are all priests, we all have access to the Holy of Holies, we all have a special place in the Body of Christ, we are all the sheep of His pasture. Therefore we love one another, respect one another and serve one another as we strive toward the same goal: obedience to our Lord and Master.

CHAPTER FIFTEEN

The Greatest Need in Today's Church

As we come to the end of our discussion of layman-pastor relationships, we realize that something more than casual effort is needed to get the job done in the church. A great many questions surge to the forefront when we seek to actually implement the advice in the previous chapters. After all, it is one thing to consider what might be done under ideal conditions, but the fact is that unless we are careful we tend to oversimplify. For example, while it is recognized that there is a pastor (chapter 1) and that he is a messenger from God (chapter 2), once we feel we have the right man and he is called to the church (chapter 3), what happens when the honeymoon is over and there are minor clashes? Perhaps they are nothing serious enough to question a pastor's position or question whether or not he should leave the church, but they are little quirks that have been discovered by the people about their pastor, and layman-quirks that the pastor has recognized as well. The problem of money matters (chapter 9) could well arise, and a Baptist church could have as many views on this as it does members.

Also, the very idea of providing the pastor with pensions, automobiles and extra conferences (chapter 11) may not set well with some members. The solutions suggested for the "little foxes" (chapter 12) could cause some resentment on the part of ushers and others who seem to rationalize their questionable church etiquette.

In other words, how do we implement these suggestions? Knowing the material—even agreeing with it—is one thing; doing it is another. Is there something that can "bring it all together" and make it work?

Climate Is Important

We believe the answer to these questions and observations is one of climate. If the church is going to maintain the kind of layman-pastor balance it needs; if there is going to be understanding and harmony between the "professional staff" and the layman, there is one ingredient that is most important. It is fair to say that without it, none of the advice given in this book will work effectively.

The Filling of the Spirit

Without a doubt, the single most important ingredient leading to the success of the early New Testament church was the fact that they were filled with the Spirit. Simply defined, the filling of the Spirit is the *control by the Spirit* in the believer's life. No wonder such progress was made between both leaders and those who were led. We cannot have proper relationships in any sphere among Christians without the filling of the Spirit.

For example, when Paul urged the church at Ephesus to maintain right relationships in the church and the home, he gave the "filling of the Spirit" as the basis. In Ephesians 5 he speaks of the husband-wife relationship (Eph. 5:22–33), and in Ephesians 6 the child-parent relationship (Eph. 6:1-4) and the servant-master relationship (Eph. 6:5-9). But the basis for the success of these relationships is found in Ephesians 5:18, "And be not drunk with wine, wherein is excess; but be filled with the Spirit" (Eph. 5:18). Paul also spoke of "Submitting yourselves one to another in the fear of God" (Eph. 5:21).

Yes, there is leadership in the home—the husband is the head—but there is also *mutual* submission. There is leadership in the church—Christ is the head and the pastor is the undershepherd—but there is *mutual* submission, and this submission is predicated on the control of the Holy Spirit. If we were Spirit filled, there would be no aggravations, no personality clashes, no long, rough business meetings resulting in hard feelings, no church splits. Yes, the filling of the Spirit is vital to the family, whether it be the family at home or the church family. Such filling results in respecting leadership and, at the same time, being mutually submissive. This may seem like quite an order; however, it is not only possible, it is expected.

Grieve Not the Spirit

The first step in the filling of the Spirit is to be sure that the Spirit is not grieved. In Ephesians 4 we read, "Let no corrupt communication proceed out of your mouth, but that which is good to the use of edifying, that it may minister grace unto the hearers. And grieve not the holy Spirit of God, whereby ye are sealed unto the day of redemption" (Eph. 4:29, 30). Paul is saying we should be careful how we speak, that we need to edify one another. Then having said "Grieve not the holy Spirit," he adds: "Let all bitterness, and wrath, and anger, and clamour, and evil speaking, be put away from you, with all malice: And be ye kind one to another, tenderhearted, forgiving one another, even as God for Christ's sake hath forgiven you. Be ye therefore followers of God as dear children: And walk in love, as Christ also hath loved us..." (Eph. 4:31–5:2a).

When there is a bitter spirit between God's people, the Spirit is grieved. It is as simple as that. How do we stop grieving Him? We are to *put away* all malice, we are to forgive, and we are to walk in love. God expects us to deal with any sin that hinders the work of the Spirit. Too many churches have people whom God is working *to* and therefore He cannot work *through* them. They have not lost the Spirit, because He is with them forever, but they have lost the *power* of the Spirit. The answer is to confess this sin to God, deal with it forthrightly, put it away, and thus stop grieving the Spirit. Once such an attitude has been attained and the church members have become mutually submissive, the suggestions in this book can be accomplished.

Quench Not the Spirit

Not only are we told to grieve not the Spirit, but we are also told to quench not the Spirit (1 Thess. 5:19). When Paul wrote this to the Thessalonians, he was writing to a real, live congregation, just like congregations today. Earlier he had written, "...warn them that are unruly, comfort the feebleminded, support the weak, be patient toward all men. See that none render evil for evil unto any man; but ever follow that which is good, both among yourselves, and to all men" (1 Thess. 5:14, 15). Do you catch the spirit of those injunctions? There may have been problems in this congregation. Some may have been unruly, some weak, some impatient, some combative. There was a variety of attitudes among them. Paul exhorts them about these attitudes, then adds, "Quench not the Spirit" (1 Thess. 5:19). What is the difference between grieving the Spirit and quenching the Spirit? Grieving seems to deal with specific sins that need to be confessed. But those who are quenching the Spirit are probably saying no to the Spirit. That is, they are "turning the Spirit down" in areas where they should be responding affirmatively to Him. It is possible to be rather bland in life so that no one can accuse us of being bitter or unruly, but at the same time we could be *ever so politely* saying no to areas of service and cooperation in the work of the church. We are still quenching the Spirit when we say no to Him, even though it might be a whisper or a very gentle decline. Too often the church is a "one-man" affair because so many are not willing to be involved in the "work of the ministry." A heart that is not grieving the Spirit (with all sin confessed) and is not quenching the Spirit (saying yes to the Spirit in areas of service) is one that has met two of the basic criteria for the Spirit's control.

Walk in the Spirit

The third and final prerequisite for the filling of the Spirit is found in the fifth chapter of Galatians: "Walk in the Spirit, and ye shall not fulfil the lust of the flesh" (Gal. 5:16). Note the order:

Grieve not the Spirit

Quench not the Spirit

Walk in the Spirit

The first two are negative, the third is positive. The first two deal with sin, the third deals with obedience in faith.

When we first learned to walk it was a thrilling experience, not only for us but for our parents. You might say that when we walked, "every step was an incipient fall." It was hard at first because every step required us to temporarily lose our balance. That was necessary in order to take a step. But once a step was taken, it soon led to another and another, and what was once initially difficult became very natural. This is also true of the church. We believe that "walking in the Spirit" is a step-by-step walk of faith. When the church, both pastor and people, begin to walk *by the Spirit* (the literal meaning of the passage),they are on their way to a balanced and fruitful ministry. No wonder the early church grew to such proportions. They stepped out in a venture of faith which included a dependence on the Lord for power and a willingness to follow Him. They were responding as members of the Body to the Head, in the power of the Spirit.

Yes, a church that is not grieving Him" (relation-ships are right between each other), a church that is not quenching Him (each member is saying yes to His promptings) and a church that is walking in Him in faith and utter dependence is a church that impacts the world for Christ. Rather than strain within the church there is gain; rather than confrontation there is cooperation; rather than a gap between pastor and people there is uni-ty and oneness. Bitterness turns into love, and declines in service are turned into a hearty willingness to be in-volved. The church becomes a partnership, and God is glorified.

Bibliography

Books

Barclay, William, *The Letters to Timothy, Titus, and Philemon.* Philadelphia: Westminster Press, 1960.

Barnhouse, Donald Grey. *Revelation: An Expository Commentary.* Grand Rapids: Zondervan Publishing House, 1971.

Criswell, W. A. *Expository Sermons on Revelation.* Vol. 2. Grand Rapids: Zondervan Publishing House, 1963.

Edwards, Jonathan. *The Works of President Edwards.* London: Leavitt, Trow and Co., 1848.

Erdman, Charles R. *The Pastoral Epistles of Paul.* Philadelphia: Westminster Press, 1923.

Getz, Gene. *Sharpening the Focus of the Church.* Chicago: Moody Press, 1974.

Gillaspie, Gerald W. *The Empty Pulpit.* Chicago: Moody Press, 1975.

Hendriksen, William. *New Testament Commentary: Exposition of the Pastoral Epistles.* Grand Rapids: Baker Book House, 1957.

Kent, Homer A. *The Pastoral Epistles of Paul.* Chicago: Moody Press, 1958.

Lenski, R. C. H. *The Interpretation of St. John's Revelation.* Columbus, OH: Wartburg Press, 1943.

Lightfoot, J. B. *Saint Paul's Epistle to the Philippians.* London: Mcmillan and Co., 1890.

Lindgren, Alvin J. *Foundations of Purposeful Church Administration.* Nashville: Abingdon Press, 1965.

Newell, William R. *The Book of the Revelation.* Chicago: Moody Press, 1935.

Scofield, C. I., ed. Scofield Reference Holy Bible. New York: Oxford Press, 1917.

Seiss, J. A. *The Apocalypse.* London: McArchall, Morgan and Scott, n. d.

Spurgeon, Charles Haddon. *Lectures to My Students.* Grand Rapids: Zondervan Publishing House, 1977.

Strong, Augustus Hopkins. *Systematic Theology.* Philadelphia: Judson Press, 1907.

Trench, Richard Chenevix. *Commentary on the Epistles to the Seven Churches in Asia.* New York: Charles Scribner, 1862.

Walvoord, John F. *The Revelation of Jesus Christ.* Chicago: Moody Press, 1966.

Wuest, Kenneth S. *The Pastoral Epistles in the Greek New Testament.* Grand Rapids: Wm. B. Eerdmans Publishing Co., 1952.

Magazines

"A Biblical Style of Leadership." *Leadership* (Spring 1981): pp. 68–77.

Holck, Manfred. *Leadership* (Winter 1980): pp. 40-41.

Mains, David. "My Greatest Ministry Mistakes." *Leadership* (Spring 1980): p. 15.

Robbins, Paul D. *Leadership* (Spring 1981): pp. 36, 42.

"Sharpening the Pastor's Focus." *Leadership* (Summer 1985): pp. 13-14.